DEC '99   6. 05

T0050586

Jesus
the Peacemaker

Carol Frances Jegen, BVM

Sheed & Ward

To
my family,
peacemakers
most precious

All Scripture quotations are taken from *The New American Bible* (New York: Thomas Nelson Publishers 1971).

Copyright © 1986
Carol Frances Jegen, BVM

All rights reserved. No part of this book may be reproduced or transmitted in any form or by any means, electronic or mechanical, including photocopying, recording or by an information storage and retrieval system without permission in writing from the Publisher.

Sheed & Ward™ is a service of National Catholic Reporter Publishing, Inc.

Library of Congress Catalog Card Number: 86-60789

ISBN: 0-934134-36-7

Published by: Sheed & Ward
   115 E. Armour Blvd. P.O. Box 414292
   Kansas City, MO 64141-0281

To order, call: (800) 821-7926

Contents

INTRODUCTION

Jesus the Peacemaker is one response to the urgent plea for a theology of peace set forth in *The Challenge of Peace*, the historic 1983 pastoral letter of the Catholic bishops of the United States. Throughout this present study, references are made to the pastoral letter's timely and prophetic message "to Catholics in the United States to join with others in shaping the conscious choices and deliberate policies required in this 'moment of supreme crisis'" (#4).

The Christological approach of *Jesus the Peacemaker* is rooted in the New Testament, including many of its considerations of the Hebraic background of Jesus of Nazareth. Two other pivotal points in history receive considerable comment: the fourth century turning point when the church moved from a predominantly peacemaking stance to one of justifying war; and the contemporary 'moment of supreme crisis' in which lies hope-filled possibilities for moving into a new peacemaking posture. Christian writers of the early church and of today's church are compared and sometimes contrasted, in an effort to ascertain the development of, or the deviation from, the Christian gospel of peacemaking.

Chapter One, "Toward a Peacemaking Christology," situates the entire study in the contexts of *The Challenge of Peace* and of contemporary Christological developments. The methodology is explained with reference to an experiential orientation, both with respect to Jesus and to peacemaking Christians, past and present. Finally, the reasons for using the passion narrative as the focal point of all deliberations is explained, along with the reasons for using the word *peacemaking* in this Christological study.

The power theology of the passion narrative is the central theme of Chapter Two, "Empowering for Peace." The power struggle in which Jesus was involved is analyzed with respect to its political ramifications in Jesus' life and also with reference to his own inner wrestling with the question of power. Jesus' confrontation with military power is studied along with references to this confrontation in the early writings of the church. The sense of power evident in the earliest Christians as indicated in Acts is considered also.

Chapter Three, "Prayer of Peacemakers," studies the prayer of Jesus in relation to peacemaking. Jesus' prayer life was influenced greatly by the Hebrew scriptures. Consequently, this chapter concentrates on the theology of prayer as found in the Isaian servant songs. The relation between prayerfulness and empowerment for justice and peace is highlighted as a needed focus in contemporary Christology.

Little attention has been given to the gift and art of play as far as theology is concerned. We rarely think of Jesus' playfulness, even in his risen life when he is most fully child of God. Genuine playfulness is a human art and has much to do with peacemaking. The fourth chapter, "Playfulness and Peacemaking," considers the art of playfulness as necessary in the process of becoming children, the Beatitudes way of describing peacemakers.

In Chapter Five, "Programming for Peace," Jesus' teachings on peacemaking are studied, using the Beatitudes and other sections from the Sermon on the Mount as the major points of reference. Various interpretations of these teachings in Christian history are treated, particularly from the period of the early Constantinian era when the church moved into a just war position. Interpretations in other periods of Christian life are included also.

4

Three preludes to peacemaking are sounded in the final sixth chapter. The Lucan infancy narrative with its strong peace motif is studied in its introductory position in the Gospel. The early peacemaking Christology of the Epistle to the Ephesians is examined as a way to begin to focus a needed peacemaking Christology in contemporary times. Finally, two sacraments of initiation, baptism and eucharist, are considered in the light of the early church Orders in their reluctance to reconcile warmaking with Christian sacramental life. These 'preludes' from scripture and sacrament call forth a peacemaking way of life, one which enables us to really know Jesus peacemaker.

To Mundelein College which provided me with a sabbatical year and to the Institute for Ecumenical and Cultural Research at St. John's University in Collegeville, Minnesota where this study originated and developed through the encouragement of the entire Institute community, I am deeply grateful.

Carol Frances Jegen, BVM

1. Toward a Peacemaking Christology

The 1983 pastoral letter of the Catholic bishops of the United States focused on peace as a challenge. This historic document, *The Challenge of Peace: God's Promise and Our Response*, includes another challenge in its request to theologians to develop a theology of peace. In the introductory section of the letter after commenting on "the religious vision of peace among peoples and nations" . . . which has "an objective basis and is capable of progressive realization,"[1] the bishops spoke of "the Church's responsibility to join with others in the work of peace" (#23). This responsibility of cooperation with all others in peacemaking efforts was named "a major force behind the call today to develop a theology of peace" (#23). This call to develop a theology of peace appears again in the final section of the document entitled, "The Pastoral Challenge and Response." In the section on Educators, we find an urgency in the message addressed to theologians. The bishops wrote, "We address theologians in a particular way, because we know that we have only begun the journey toward a theology of peace; without your specific contributions this desperately needed dimension of our faith will not be realized. Through your help we may provide a new vision and wisdom for church and state" (#304).

This challenge to develop a theology of peace recurs with greater specificity when the bishops refer to the Second Vatican Council's challenge "to undertake a completely fresh reappraisal of war" (#23). Significantly, two kinds of sources are men-

5

tioned as needed contributions for a developed theology of peace: various branches of theology, including biblical studies, systematic and moral theology, and ecclesiology; and the experience and insights of peacemaking Christians (#24). One would expect that theological sources would be considered necessary material for new theological development. What is surprising and very welcome in this request is the seriousness with which the *experience of Christians* is considered a primary source for a theology of peace.

Not only in scripture studies do we find renewed emphasis on the experience of the primitive Christian community as a key to understanding the Gospels, but in the other areas of theological studies as well, we are becoming more aware of the indispensable grounding of all theological reflection in the faith experience of Christians. This emphasis on experience resonates clearly with theological awareness on the part of more and more scholars, influenced by theological giants such as Lonergan and Schillebeeckx. Liberation theologians consider a praxis/experience foundation basic to all their theology. This experience aspect of contemporary theological method implies peacemaking involvement as a necessary background for theological understanding of the Christian imperative to make peace. Consequently, in this present development of a peacemaking Christology, the experience of peacemaking will serve as a touchstone of genuine theological insight.

As the bishops conclude their plea for a theology of peace, they admit to having "some sense of the characteristics of a theology of peace, but not a systematic statement of their relationships" (#24). Developing a systematic synthesis of all the facets of a theology of peace is a gigantic undertaking, one encompassing all the aspects of Christian life as that life is reflected in worship and in social action as well as in theological thought. The unifying factor in such a systematic development can be a Christology, one which clarifies peace and peacemaking as central in the concerns and works of Jesus, including his passion, death and resurrection. Such a peacemaking Christology will highlight the experience of Jesus as peacemaker, and will resonate with the experience of today's peacemaking Christians and with the experiences of Christians in other periods of the church's life who, in their efforts for making peace, were faithful and often heroic even unto martyrdom.

The correlation between peacemaking and Christological understanding and emphasis in any given period of history raises crucial questions about the church's role in warmaking and in peacemaking. A peacemaking Christology will call into question some of the attitudes and practices of Christians during the past 1600 years, in which our predominant posture as a church has been one of "justifying war." A vital Christology, speaking clearly to the pastoral needs of the nuclear age, can greatly influence the Christian peacemaker, who must be sustained in wisdom, courage, and self-sacrificing love. Also, such a peacemaking Christology can be very instrumental in the conversion process so necessary in the Christian community as we wrestle with the consequences of violence, a violence which has accelerated to global proportions and for which we bear grave responsibility in our war-scarred history.

In *The Challenge of Peace*, two scriptural sections on "Jesus and the Reign of God" and "Jesus and the Community of Believers" are situated within a Christological frame of reference, if one considers the document in its entirety. The second paragraph and the final paragraph serve as a framework placing the entire pastoral in a faith perspective centered on Jesus. Paragraph two claims, "Faith does not insulate us from the challenges of life; rather, it intensifies our desire to help solve them precisely in the light of the good news which has come to us in the person of Jesus, the Lord of history." This reference to Jesus as the Lord of history gives a Christological orientation to the entire document, an orientation which is rooted in Israel's awareness of God's saving acts in history. The last paragraph of the pastoral proclaims, "It is our belief in the risen Christ which sustains us in confronting the awesome challenge of the nuclear arms race. Present in the beginning as the word of the Father, present in history as the word incarnate, and with us today in his word, sacraments, and spirit, he is the reason for our hope and faith. Respecting our freedom, he does not solve our problems but sustains us as we take responsibility for his work of creation and try to shape it in the ways of the kingdom. We believe his grace will never fail us" (#339).

In addition to these introductory and concluding paragraphs of the peace pastoral, the section on prayer reminds us, "in prayer we encounter Jesus who is our peace and learn from him the way to peace" (#290). And when, in the concluding section of the pastoral, the bishops teach that "peacemaking is not an optional commitment" but a "requirement of our faith," they state emphatically, "We are called to be peacemakers, not by some movement of the moment, but by our Lord Jesus" (#333).

By way of introduction to this study of a peacemaking Christology, one other reference to Jesus found in the peace pastoral deserves special mention now, and more extensive treatment later. The Ephesians text (Eph.2:12-18) identifying Jesus as our peace because he has made peace through his death on the cross is the first direct scriptural reference in the pastoral (#20). This text, one of the early Christological statements of the New Testament, is profoundly rich in its interweaving of covenant theology, eucharistic theology, and a theology of reconciliation. It also emphasizes the integral relation between peacemaking and peace.

These references to Jesus found throughout *The Challenge of Peace* point to the need for further theological development in the area of Christology, even though Christology was not mentioned explicitly in the paragraph listing various branches of theology which will contribute to a developed theology of peace (#24). From the standpoint of theological disciplines, surely Christology was intended in the mention of systematic theology and implied indirectly in the explicit reference to ecclesiology.

But even if the peace pastoral had not been written, the perilous condition of the human race in its present situation of nuclear madness calls for a reawakening on the part of all

Christians to the meaning of Jesus, whom we believe is the savior of the world. Does such a statement of faith, savior of the world, have any bearing on the world in which we live, a planet threatened with the destruction of all its living creatures? What wisdom can we find in Jesus' ways of making peace? What power of Jesus can we depend on as we face today's struggle with demonic powers of unimaginable violence?

This beginning development of a peacemaking Christology comes on the scene in this "moment of supreme crisis"[2] after extensive theological work on Jesus has been accomplished in an amazingly brief period of time. All one has to do is to consult bibliographical listings of the past decade or so to become aware of the vast amount of scholarly work on Jesus that has been accomplished in our day.[3] The works of three contemporary theologians have exerted considerable influence on this present study: Jon Sobrino's *Christology at the Crossroads*; Monika Hellwig's *Jesus the Compassion of God*; and *Above Every Name, the Lordship of Christ and Social Systems*, edited by Thomas E. Clarke.[4] Each of these recent Christological treatises, developed in the Americas, has emphasized the experience of Jesus and has helped locate that experience in relation to our world situation. Each work has opened the way for a needed emphasis on a new Christology of peacemaking.

In his Preface to the English edition of *Christology at the Crossroads*, Jon Sobrino makes several observations which are critical for approaching any Christological study. Sobrino urges a threefold suspicion. First of all, Christ must not be reduced to a sublime abstraction, which separates the Christ of faith from the Jesus of history. Secondly, an emphasis on the eschatological truth of Christ as an embodiment of universal reconciliation (an emphasis extremely important in a peacemaking Christology) must never ignore the historical sin which actually caused the death of Jesus. In this context Sobrino warns against the use of Christianity as an ideology for promoting a situation of order and peace which flies in the face of justice. Such an ideology, supported by a false Christology, can encourage and engineer flagrant and cruel violations of basic human rights in the attainment of a so-called ordered peace. Thirdly, Sobrino cautions against a process of absolutizing Christ as the ultimate value in life in such a way that the real needs of human living are downplayed and even totally ignored. In such distorted Christologies, the significance of history, of real life experiences, both Jesus' and ours, is undermined with devastating effects, especially for the world's poor and oppressed.

The Preface to the original Spanish edition, *Cristologia desde America Latina*, speaks to the irrelevance of traditional European Christologies as far as Latin America is concerned. From his experience in El Salvador, Sobrino knows that a meaningful Christology must be rooted in the historical Jesus and in the history of a people's pain and sorrow. In other words, in the experience of Jesus, Christians must find meaning in their own experience. In simple Christological terms, Jesus must make all the difference in peoples' lives. In Jesus, people must be able to recognize God's definitive salvific action for the entire human family.

Time and again, throughout the entire volume, Sobrino shares his conviction that the only way to know Jesus is to follow him in one's own life. In relation to the strong experiential emphasis of Sobrino's work, chapter four on "The Faith of Jesus" is most insightful. Cautioning against an over-emphasis on isolated events in Jesus' life, Sobrino insists on the total historical movement of Jesus' life as the key to the revelation of who Jesus is and what Jesus means in human history as the Christ, the anointed one of God. In Jesus' faith-vision of life, which developed as Jesus struggled to be faithful to the God he experienced so intimately, today's Christians can discover their own way to God and to the realization of the reign of God. The faith-filled history making of today shares in and continues Jesus' own faith-filled fashioning of history. The power of God within Jesus continues to empower Christians who, in sharing Jesus' life, share likewise in a genuine growth of faith.

Monika Hellwig in her masterful treatise, *Jesus the Compassion of God*, follows Sobrino's approach as she highlights compassion as the key to understanding who Jesus is and what difference he continues to make in the world. In her characteristic openness to new questions, this theologian claims that "the new discussions should deal with new matter that was not a subject of the classic formulations, such as the relationship of the Incarnation and Resurrection to the practical possibility of permanent peace in the world."[5] Not only in this specific reference to a possible peacemaking orientation to Christology, but also in her characteristic treatment of theology as an art in which truth can be recognized by "the harmony of beauty, of consolation, of purpose in life, of challenge"[6] does Monika Hellwig make room for and encourage the development of a peacemaking Christology.

In her final chapter on "Jesus and Gandhi: Salvation and Non-violence," the claim is made that Gandhi may have understood Jesus better than most Christians ever will. The reason for this claim is the harmony of Gandhi's experience and Jesus' experience with respect to great intimacy with God and limitless compassion for people. This compassionate way of life is of necessity expressed in non-violence. The entire book concludes with an emphatic proclamation of faith in the power of the risen Jesus, incarnate Compassion of God, at work in today's non-violent efforts. "This is perhaps the clearest sign that Christ is risen and is among us, for the incarnate Compassion of God is most appropriately and powerfully expressed in non-violent action for justice and peace in the world."[7]

Monika Hellwig's essay, "Christology and Attitudes Toward Social Structures," begins the excellent volume *Above Every Name*, in which eleven theologians wrestle with the implications of the lordship of Jesus for today's society and culture. In introducing the book, editor Thomas Clarke explains that lordship is "the most germane Christological term for regarding the Christian faith in relation to social systems"[8] because the term *lord* relates most readily to the theme of power, that reality of primary concern in any consideration of societal justice and peace. The final essay of John Farrelly discusses "The Peace of Christ in the Earthly City." This essay, relying heavily on recent interpretations of Lucan theology, focuses on the realistic possibilities for peace in human society. Christian fidelity to the basic teachings of Jesus regarding one's relation to other persons and peoples as well as one's relation to God is considered in its transformative power for societal peace.

In reflecting on the societal thrust of these contemporary Christological developments with respect to the development of a peacemaking Christology, well might the question be raised as to whether peacemaking is a key to Christology or the other way around. Perhaps it is more accurate to approach Christology as key to peacemaking. Considering the recent rediscovery of the fact that faith experience is a necessary prerequisite for the writing of the Gospels and also for all subsequent life-giving theology, it would seem to be more accurate to say that peacemaking is key to Christology. However, such a claim does not deny the fact that a peacemaking Christology can do much to enlighten, encourage and sustain Christians engaged in a variety of efforts for making peace. On the contrary, a peacemaking Christology can play a vital role in today's challenge of peace.

A peacemaking Christology can find some of its experience data in the lives of all Christians who suffered and even died rather than participate in war. From the young martyr Maximilian, the first known conscientious objector of the third century,[9] to Franz Jaegerstaetter, the Austrian peasant who was put to death because of his refusal to participate in Hitler's wars,[10] to the Christian conscientious objectors of our own day, there is much to be pondered regarding the testimony of these Christians to the meaning of Jesus in their lives.

We have already referred to the peace pastoral's insistence on learning from the "experience and insights of members of the Church who have struggled in various ways to make and keep the peace in this often violent age" (#24). But no life could speak more loudly or clearly about peace and peacemaking than the life of Jesus. A peacemaking Christology, like any other particular emphasis in Christological development, must begin with the experience of Jesus, peacemaker, as we can know that experience from the Gospels.

Recent scripture scholarship has helped us understand how the passion narrative is the focal point of the Gospel. This fact indicates that the early Christian communities began to develop some of their various Christologies by reflecting on the profound mystery of Jesus' passion, death and resurrection. Therein could be found the answer to their question and ours, What difference does Jesus make? This question is the basis for all Christology insofar as it does not separate the saving work of Jesus from the person of Jesus. In regard to a peacemaking Christology, the question then becomes, What difference does Jesus make in approaching the challenge of peacemaking in a nuclear age?

Because Jesus had entered into the mystery of human suffering; because Jesus had undergone the agony of a cruel death; and because the earliest Christians witnessed to the presence of the risen Jesus in their midst, those same Christians knew the good news about Jesus had to be proclaimed. Jesus really made all the difference *in* the world, in their world agonizing under political oppression and yearning for peace. Jesus made all the difference *for* the world, theirs and ours, as we take seriously his own ways for making peace.

The passion narratives were not proclaimed in abstract theological concepts, however. They were written as genuine narratives, as eyewitness accounts of a real human experience on the part of Jesus and on the part of many other persons as well. Entering into and reflecting on this genuine human experience of suffering, death, and entry into risen life were the necessary prerequisities for the church to speak of the power of the paschal mystery. One could readily ask another question. Without the persecution and sufferings and martyrdoms which began in the earliest years of the church's life, could the Gospels have been written? For the kind of insight into the meaning of human life which the Gospel proclaims, was not the sharing of the experience of Jesus' suffering and death a necessity?

Could anything less than a love strong enough to "fill up what was lacking in the sufferings of Christ for his body the church" (Col.1:24) have enabled those earliest Christian communities to really understand Jesus well enough to proclaim his Gospel and eventually to write it?

The passion narrative still remains the focal point of the Gospel. Today as we Christians turn to Jesus whom we have learned to call Lord of History, our questions may seem to be quite different from those of the early Christians. Quite obviously, the passion narrative says nothing directly about averting a nuclear holocaust. But is the underlying issue of death transformed into life, which the Gospel proclaims, really that different? Jesus was put to death in a cruel, violent way by the superpower of his day, the Roman Empire. He suffered a cowardly betrayal for the sake of money. He was the victim of a deceptive compromise on the part of some of his own religious authorities, blinded by their internal power struggles. Precisely in all this sinful, human conniving, Jesus, incarnate wisdom, witnessed to God's own radical ways of making the way for genuine peace, a peace for this world as well as the next.

In order to see more clearly Jesus' strategy for peacemaking, we must look at the whole passion narrative from the Last Supper account through to the mystery of Pentecost. Then we may turn to the rest of the Gospel and see with new vision the meaning of Jesus' teachings on the making of peace. Approaching the Gospel in this way, we will be following the pattern of the Gospel's composition. Following this pattern of study, we will be able to understand better why the infancy narrative of the Lucan Gospel, one of the final sections to be written, promises in the canticle of Zachary, almost by way of keynote, that Jesus will "guide our feet into the way of peace" (Lk.1:79).

Drawing wisdom and courage and hope from the passion narrative of Jesus presupposes a certain commonality of experience. A Church in persecution gave us the New Testament. In the words of the peace pastoral, "As believers we can identify rather easily with the early Church as a company of witnesses engaged in a difficult mission . . . To set out on the road to discipleship is to dispose oneself for a share in the cross (cf.Jn.16:20) . . . We must regard as normal even the path of persecution and the possibility of martyrdom" (#276).

Insofar as we can enter with compassion into the suffering of our own time, we can discover the wisdom of the Gospel. Has any other century known such widespread suffering as ours? Whether it be the direct ravages of recent wars — Holocaust victims, Hiroshima and Nagasaki and all bombing victims, soldiers in veterans hospitals all over the world, war orphans and widows; or today's millions suffering economic exploitation and starvation because of the arms race; or those in prison in our own country or elsewhere because of their non-violent protests against warmaking policies and practices; or the increasing numbers of refugees from wartorn countries; or the crippling psychological damage, especially to our youth, caused by the impending threat of nuclear disaster; or the hidden weariness and exhaustion of those most involved in peacemaking efforts, often in the face of apathy, resistance, and even hostility — today, to be alive at all as a Christian means to be a member of a suffering people. Our challenge is to be a people suffering in compassionate ways. Then, we can share human life united in Jesus and know the transforming power of his love. In the light of this shared experience, we can understand the Gospel's call to peacemaking.

The Synod of 1971 gave us that remarkable statement, "Action on behalf of justice and participation in the transformation of the world fully appear to us as a constitutive dimension of the preaching of the Gospel . . . "[11] The primary thrust of this declaration is on action as a way of *proclaiming* the Gospel. What may not be as readily apparent is this statement's implication that action is a necessary way of *understanding* the Gospel.

On this note of action, one final distinction is in order with respect to the term *peacemaking*, clearly an action word. Rather than designate this present study as a peace Christology, after considerable reflection I have opted for a peacemaking Christology instead. Perhaps the subtitle of the peace pastoral can be helpful in understanding the distinction as well as the relation between peacemaking and peace. The subtitle, *God's Promise and Our Response*, reminds us that peace is a promised gift of God. Commenting on this promised gift of God, the pastoral refers briefly to various meanings for peace: an individual's sense of well-being or security; cessation of armed hostility; a right relationship with God, entailing forgiveness, reconciliation, and union; and eschatological peace.

The second phrase of the pastoral's subtitle, *Our Response*, puts the emphasis on our responsibility for peacemaking. Peacemaking depends in no small way on the peace of God received and cherished in one's mind and heart. This interior peace, fruit of a loving relationship with God, enables us to enter into God's own compassionate ways of making peace. The term *peacemaking* challenges us to action and helps dispel the notion of passivity and isolated sectarianism often associated with certain forms of pacifism. Peacemaker is Beatitude language and points to the mystery of becoming true children of God in union with God's own Son, Jesus who is peacemaker *par excellence*.

Peacemaking can be considered in two ways: either as a way of preventing conflict, or as a way of reconciliation after conflict has occurred. Lessons learned through the experience of genuine reconciliation can be helpful in staving off pending conflict through peacemaking approaches. With respect to nuclear war, peacemaking must precede the potential conflict because of the obvious reason that there will be no opportunity to make peace in the wake of global disaster. Prevention of nuclear war is the primary challenge of peacemaking in our time, and we in the United States have the major responsibility to accomplish it because we are engaged in warmaking preparations beyond human description. In the words of the pastoral, "As Americans, citizens of the nation which was the first to produce atomic weapons, which has been the only one to use them and which today is one of the handful of nations capable of decisively influencing the course of the nuclear age, we have grave human, moral and political responsibilities to see that a 'conscious choice' is made to save humanity" (#4).

This peacemaking Christology, concentrating heavily on the Gospel passion narratives as key to understanding all of the peacemaking actions and teachings of Jesus, can be classified as an Easter Christology, according to Schillebeeckx's helpful designations.[12] Such a Christology centers on the passion, death, and resurrection of Jesus wherein the Christian community experiences God's transforming action in history and is empowered to continue that same transforming work through, with, and in the risen Jesus. Easter Christologies are Christologies of hope. May this study be hope-giving to all Christians facing the challenge of peacemaking.

Footnotes

[1] National Conference of Catholic Bishops, *The Challenge of Peace: God's Promise and Our Response* (Washington, DC, U.S.C.C. 1983) #20.

[2] The Introduction to *The Challenge of Peace* begins with the Second Vatican Council's opening statement in its treatment of modern warfare: "The whole human race faces a moment of supreme crisis in its advance toward maturity" (*The Church in the Modern World,* #77).

[3] Cf. Bernard Cooke, "Horizons on Christology in the Seventies," *Horizons* 6/2 (1979) 193-217. Also see Monika Hellwig, *Jesus the Compassion of God* (Wilmington: Michael Glazier 1983), "Introduction: The Present State of the Question in the Theoretical Structure of Christology" and Chapter 1, "Christian Questions About Jesus."

[4] Jon Sobrino, *Christology at the Crossroads*, tr. John Drury (Maryknoll: Orbis 1978); Monika Hellwig, see note 3 above; Thomas E. Clarke, ed., *Above Every Name* (New York: Paulist 1980).

[5] Hellwig, *Jesus*, p. 13.

[6] Hellwig, *Jesus*, p. 15.

[7] Hellwig, *Jesus*, p. 155.

[8] Clarke, *Above*, p. 3.

[9] Maximilian's powerful testimony to Jesus as recorded in the *Acts of Martyrs* is quoted in Louis J. Swift, *The Early Fathers on War and Military Service* (Wilmington: Michael Glazier 1983) p. 72f.

[10] For a brief account of this contemporary martyr, see Gordon Zahn, *Franz*

Jaegerstaetter, Martyr for Conscience (Erie, Pa: Benet Press 1985 reprint). For more information than this booklet provides, see Gordon Zahn, *In Solitary Witness: The Life and Death of Franz Jaegerstaetter* (Boston: Beacon Press 1968).

[11] Second Synod of Bishops, "Justice in the World," 6, as given in Joseph Gremillion, ed., *The Gospel of Peace and Justice. Catholic Social Teaching Since Pope John XXIII* (Maryknoll: Orbis 1976).

[12] For Schillebeeckx, an Easter Christology is one aspect of his insight into Jesus as the eschatological prophet. For a helpful introduction to this basic Christological motif of Schillebeeckx, see Robert Schreiter, ed., *The Schillebeeckx Reader* (New York: Crossroad 1984) p. 164f. Also see Edward Schillebeeckx, *Interim Report on the Books Jesus & Christ*, tr. John Bowden (New York: Crossroad 1981), ch. 5, "Fundamental Points for Discussion."

2. Empowering for Peace

The question of power and empowerment is a major theme in the passion narratives. Chronologically speaking, John's account of Jesus washing the feet of his disciples is the first episode of the story. There are many ways to consider this amazing scene of Jesus performing such a menial task. Clearly this action of Jesus speaks a message of selfless service in love. When this action is considered in the light of the supper dialog in the Lucan account, we can see also something of Jesus' ideas on the role of leadership for those in authority positions who are entrusted with power. In the context of a dispute about who should be regarded as the greatest, Luke gives us the response of Jesus. "Earthly kings lord it over their people. Those who exercise authority over them are called their benefactors. Yet it cannot be that way with you . . . " (Lk. 22:25f).

It is not too difficult to relate this teaching on the use of authority to the question of peace and peacemaking. The history of the human family is brutally scarred by those in authority seeking more and more power and using more and more violent means to secure their power positions. How totally opposite is Jesus' action and teaching here in the context of the last supper. When Jesus washing the feet of his disciples is seen in relation to their arguing about who was the greatest, a direct message of peacemaking becomes apparent. Not only does Jesus revolutionize the meaning of authority and power, he also witnesses to his own teachings on the forgiveness of enemies by performing this gesture of love.

What is highly significant here is that the act of forgiveness is inserted into a scene which focuses on authority and power. The passion narratives make it quite clear Jesus knew his disciples' weaknesses. He was aware of a pending betrayal, of a cowardly denial, and of a wholesale flight in fear. In just a few hours, his chosen friends, his future leaders, would act like his enemies. Might they have remained enemies without Jesus' immediate gesture of forgiving love?

Much more emphasis on forgiveness is included in the passion accounts and will be considered later in this study. But this particular action, one which could be interpreted as an act of anticipatory forgiveness, needs to be pondered in the context of authority and power. In washing the feet of his chosen leaders who would soon abandon him, Jesus was loving his enemies. He wanted to be sure his action was understood, so he asked, "Do you understand what I just did for you?" (Jn. 13:12). Referring to the titles Teacher and Lord, titles resplendent with power meanings, Jesus directed his future leaders to follow his example of lowly service and forgiveness. He promised, "Once you know all these things, blest will you be if you put them into practice" (Jn. 13:17). Here, at the beginning of his passion, Jesus was changing radically the meaning of lordship and the exercise of power. Jesus was illustrating ways of peacemaking for those in authority positions.

In commenting on this scene from the passion narrative, William Klassen, in his insightful study *Love of Enemies*, makes several observations on Luke's treatment of power in relation to John's. Luke's concern about the structure of human relationships influences greatly his emphasis on the new power structures which Jesus' disciples will foster as peacemakers. As Luke continues to relate Jesus' supper discourse and includes the fact that Jesus assigns the "dominion" of his Father to the apostles, the implications of such an assignment are clear. Those in authority are to follow in the way Jesus had shown them. In Klassen's words, "This method of ruling eliminates the power struggle and sets its highest premium on the way in which one serves the neighbor."[1]

The Lucan Gospel relates authoritative power to peacemaking in the description of Jesus entering Jerusalem. Considering Luke's theological use of geography,[2] this scene is a climactic one. This Gospel makes it clear that Jesus' whole ministry would culminate in Jerusalem. Furthermore, Jesus knew he would suffer there. Luke's transfiguration account mentions Jerusalem explicitly as the place where Jesus knew his "passage" would be fulfilled (Lk. 9:31).

Jesus experienced an exuberant crowd as he descended on a donkey from Mount Olivet toward Jerusalem. When Matthew describes this scene, in his customary way he relates Jesus' action to a prophecy from the Hebrew scriptures. "Tell the daughter of Zion, your king comes to you without display astride an ass, astride a colt, the foal of a beast of burden" (Mt. 21:5; Ze. 9:9). This description of a meek king who is a just savior is followed immediately in Zechariah's prophetic announcement by a passage describing disarmament and proclaiming peace.

> He shall banish the chariot from Ephraim,
>   and the horse from Jerusalem;
> The warrior's bow shall be banished,
>   and he shall proclaim peace to the nations.
> His dominion shall be from sea to sea,
>   and from the River to the ends of the earth (Ze. 9:10).

What a striking contrast to the Roman rulers proudly displaying their war horses is presented here for the people of Jerusalem! Jesus, proclaimer of peace, comes on a donkey, without any weapons of war or displays of military might. Yet the crowd recognized power in Jesus and began to rejoice. Luke tells us, "The entire crowd of disciples began to rejoice and praise God loudly for the display of power they had seen . . . " (Lk. 19:37). Their exclamations resounded: "Blessed is he who comes as king in the name of the Lord! Peace in heaven and glory in the highest" (Lk. 19:38).

The refrain, "peace in heaven and glory in the highest," obviously is reminiscent of the angels' nativity song as presented in the Lucan infancy narrative. A significant contrast is apparent however. The angels sang of peace on earth; this rejoicing crowd exclaims peace in heaven. In commenting on this Lucan doublet, Klassen follows the thinking of Raymond Brown and remarks that "the disciples recognized and publicly acknowledged what the angels declared in the theophany of Luke 2: the presence of the messianic king."[3] Klassen then adds the important comment that this entire scene of Jesus entering Jerusalem highlights the establishment of peace in heaven and on earth as an expression of Jesus' messianic kingship. Jesus' messianic identity is intrinsically related to the establishment of peace. Jesus, messiah, is peacemaker.

This peacemaking theme continues as Luke gives us one of the most touching scenes of his Gospel. Jesus is pictured weeping over Jerusalem. His reasons for weeping are tragic ones. "If only you had known the path to peace this day; but you have completely lost it from view" (Lk. 19:24). In an earlier passage, Luke pictures Jesus lamenting over Jerusalem and uses a motherly image to express his compassionate concern. "How often have I wanted to gather your children together as a mother bird collects her young under her wings, and you refused me" (Lk. 13:34). In both passages, pending destruction is the cause for lamentation and weeping — an abandoned temple, a city with its entire population destroyed, not a stone left on a stone.

"If only you had known the path to peace this day." For this reason Jesus wept. In the Lucan Gospel, immediately after this scene, Jesus entered the temple, the house of prayer, which at that point had been desecrated into a den of thieves. Luke states quite simply and succinctly, "Then he entered the temple and began ejecting the traders" (Lk. 19:45).

Because this Gospel incident is often misused to illustrate Jesus' apparent condoning of violence, this cleansing of the temple demands careful scrutiny in a study of Jesus, peacemaker. In Lucan theology, the temple plays a central role with its identity as the place of God's special presence. Jesus had to cleanse the temple because its commercial trafficking distorted severely the whole tenor of Israel's authentic worship of God. Jesus knew that through these corrupt business enterprises, the roots of violence and destruction were inserted insidiously into the holy ground which was meant to be the source of peace and life. The blatant display of money-making connivings, those business deals so often transacted at the expense of the poor who came to pray, seriously obscured the image of the God of Jesus. No wonder Jesus had wept as he faced Israel's rejection of his ways of peace. No wonder he went into action as he faced the implications of this distortion of worship. Jesus knew that authentic worship was essential for the peacemaking way of life he came to fulfill. If the worship patterns of his people were not conducive to encountering the God of compassion and selfless giving, then the possibilities for genuine peacemaking on the part of the people of God would be hopelessly curtailed.

Can this episode of temple cleansing be interpreted validly as an incident in which Jesus used violence, thereby justifying violence on the part of his disciples? In a recent essay entitled, "Power and the Pursuit of Peace: Some Reflections," John Pawlikowski refers to Jesus' "invasion of the Temple" as a Gospel incident which illustrates the need for an occasional use of destructive violence.[4] After commenting on this welcome acknowledgment of the confrontational side of Jesus as mentioned in the peace pastoral, the essay argues that "neglect of this activist and confrontational side of Jesus' ministry may well result in an overevaluation of passive resistance as the only valid model for a theology of peace."[5]

In responding to this opinion, I would question the term "invasion" as an accurate description of Jesus' action in the temple. In the light of today's experience of invasions, whether they be Vietnam, Afghanistan, or Grenada, to speak of Jesus invading the temple seems a strange exaggeration. Secondly, I would question the passivity implied in the objection to nonviolent resistance. In today's peace efforts, nonviolent resistance is usually based to some extent on the model of Gandhi. Such nonviolent resistance to evil is always very active and is in harmony with the active resistance to evil on the part of Jesus. Klassen describes the temple cleansing as "the best illustration of a 'militant nonviolent' tactic."[6] He then comments further on the lack of justification this episode provides for armed intervention of any kind.

In the fourth century, Augustine used this text in an unfortunate way as part of his apologetic for justifying war and other forms of violence. In a letter written in response to the Donatist bishop, Petilianus, Augustine's rhetorical device of parallelism and contrast might be praised, but his remarks on Jesus demand refutation. Augustine wrote, "Godless men have killed the prophets, and prophets have slain the godless; the Jews have scourged Christ and Christ has scourged the Jews."[7]

Augustine gives other examples and then explains that different motivations either justify or condemn the comparable actions. Not only in this letter, but on many other occasions, Augustine justified violence if the motive behind the violence was love for the person or persons who needed to be restrained or punished. The devastating influence of this moral reasoning is hard to estimate when one considers the subsequent history of justifying violence and warfare on the part of Christians, provided their motives were "loving."

Contrary to Augustine's interpretation of the Johannine account of the temple cleansing, a careful reading of the text pictures Jesus driving only the animals with some kind of corded whip, a rather common way to get certain animals, such as cows, to move. Jesus did not strike any persons, much less scourge them. In his classic work, *The Early Christian Attitude Toward War*, John Cadoux indicates the action of Jesus in all four Gospel accounts of this temple cleansing is described by the same Greek word, *ekballo*, meaning to cast out. Jesus was always very clear about the power able to cast out evil. It was not the power of physical force and violence, but the power of God at work within him.

Military Power

Throughout the entire passion Jesus was very aware of the abuse of power, including military power. Considering the circumstances in the Gethsemane scene, the amount of military power leveled against Jesus was absurd. However, as we know only too well in our own day, military power has an insidious way of masking its weakness under more and more weapons of violence. In the face of such power, each synoptic account relates Jesus' proclamation of another power, the power of his Father. In testimony before his own Jewish people, familiar with the Son of Man image from the Book of Daniel, Jesus responds to their questions about his identity by referring to the "Son of Man seated at the right hand of the Power and coming on the clouds of heaven" (Mt. 26:64; Mk. 14:62; Lk. 22:69). John relates Jesus' dialog with the civil authority of Rome. When Pilate flaunted his power to either release or crucify Jesus, this representative of imperial Rome was told, "You would have no power over me whatever unless it were given you from above" (Jn. 19:11).

To understand something of Jesus' fearlessness in confronting the abusive powers of his day, and his unfaltering confidence in the power of God, we must turn to the Marcan account of the agony in the garden. In Mark's account of this crucial prayer experience of Jesus, we read, "He kept saying, 'Abba (O Father) you have the power to do all things. Take this cup away from me. But let it be as you would have it, not as I'" (Mk. 14:36).

The power struggle going on in Jesus during this unspeakable agony probably finds its precedent in the desert struggle as we know it from the synoptic accounts.[9] Led into the wilderness by the Holy Spirit, Jesus had to come to grips with the question of power before he could begin his public ministry. He had to face up to the drastic differences between the abuse of power

according to the ways of sin, and the use of power according to
the way of his Abba, his Father, whose love he knew as no
other human person ever could. In the desert Jesus grew in
his conviction that the power of his Father would never be
found in material display and spectacular ways of force. God's
power was different. God's power was healing love. God's power
was suffering love.

At the end of the desert scene Luke adds, "When the devil
had finished all the tempting he left him, to await another
opportunity" (Lk. 4:13). For Luke, Jesus' struggle with contrasting ways of power was not a one-time affair. The struggle continued throughout his life and probably reached climactic proportions during Jesus' agony. Strengthened in prayer, as Jesus
entered into direct confrontation with the abusive powers of
Jerusalem and Rome, his proclamation of his Father's way of
power was a fearless one.

Particularly in the face of military might did Jesus proclaim
and exercise the power of his Father. Immediately after the
agony in the garden, Jesus was faced with a crowd carrying
swords and clubs. Peter was responsible for the first act of
physical violence in this scene when he drew his sword and cut
off the ear of the high priest's slave. Jesus' response to this
violence was to perform his final healing miracle. To refer to
this episode as the final healing miracle of Jesus at first sight
might seem to focus attention on the wounded ear which Jesus
healed. But the deeper healing involved in this scene was the
inner healing of a disciple who apparently, under circumstances
which cried out for the defense of the innocent, saw no problem
in inflicting suffering on another person by means of a violent
weapon.

It is almost belaboring the obvious to point out that Jesus
healed this violently inflicted wound as he himself was about
to suffer unbelievably cruel woundings in his own body, the
same body which had just been given up in eucharistic sacrifice.
Before describing this scene, John highlights the power of Jesus'
person. After Jesus calmly stepped forward and identified him-

self to the crowd, John tells us, "they retreated slightly and fell to the ground" (Jn. 18:6). Matthew concludes the episode with Jesus' strong, clear injunction to Peter. "Put back your sword where it belongs. Those who use the sword are sooner or later destroyed by it" (Mt. 26:52).

Probably, if we asked most Christians to mention a healing miracle of Jesus, this one from the passion narrative would not come to mind as readily as some of the others — the man born blind, the paralytic, Jairus' daughter, the centurion's servant, etc. But in our time, with our critical call to peacemaking, a process which necessitates a cessation of warmaking, I suggest we highlight this miracle of Jesus as did the Christians who lived in the first three centuries when the predominant stance of the Church was against military involvement. This healing miracle speaks with unmistakable clarity about Jesus' understanding and use of power. In contemporary language, this scene helps us comprehend something of Jesus' commitment to nonviolence.

In the pre-Constantinian era no one spoke more emphatically about the significance of this action of Jesus than Tertullian. To this day his strong statement is repeated by Christians convinced of the nonviolent stance of Jesus. Tertullian minced no words commenting on the Gethsemane text in his treatise, *On Idolatry*. Straightforwardly, he posed the question,

> Indeed how will he (a Christian) serve in the army even during peacetime without the sword that Jesus Christ has taken away? Even if soldiers came to John and got advice on how they ought to act, even if the centurion became a believer, the Lord, by taking away Peter's sword, disarmed every soldier thereafter. We are not allowed to wear the uniform that symbolizes a sinful act.[10]

Tertullian was not oblivious of the contentions of others who attempted to justify military violence by reference to the many texts in the Hebrew scriptures referring to the Israelites at war. Already in Tertullian's day some Christians appealed to such scriptural evidence to justify their military service. Precisely in the context of Jesus' Hebraic background, Tertullian made his claim that Jesus' action without any ambiguity or equivocation spoke against military violence. In the light of contemporary exegesis of the Hebrew scriptures, exegesis which is clarifying the theology of a warrior god,[11] illustrating the exaggeration of many of Israel's war accounts, and highlighting the prophetic denunciations of war,[12] Tertullian's basic insight into Jesus' repudiation of military violence could be considered a fulfillment of the Mosaic law by Jesus.

The climactic, nonviolent, healing action of Jesus in Gethsemane can be considered also as a prophetic action, perhaps even a paradigmatic one, verifying the prophetic teachings of Jesus on love and forgiveness. Tertullian claimed love of enemies was the Gospel's principal precept.[13] This Gospel spirituality of peacemaking through forgiveness and love is of prime importance in understanding the early Christian objection to war. Idolatrous practices imposed on soldiers in the Roman army were not the underlying reasons which prohibited military service. The early Christians simply could not reconcile the Gospel of Jesus with military violence, including the police duties of soldiers which often demanded brutal punishments and tortures of prisoners. Tertullian was not alone in his strong condemnation of military violence. Justin, Athenagoras, Clement of Alexandria, Origen, and Cyprian of Carthage were among the early patristic writers who found warmaking incompatible with the teachings and example of Jesus.[14]

A New Empowering

In the mystery of his passion, death, and resurrection, Jesus witnessed to a new empowering by God. The ways of abusive political power and the ways of military violence and coercion were confronted, withstood, and overcome. Throughout his passion Jesus gave testimony to the power from on high, the power of God. This was the new power promised to his disciples. The transforming power evident in the risen Jesus had broken the power of death and all that leads to death. Such was the growing faith realization of the first disciples.

In the Lucan account of Jesus' final Easter apparition to his apostles, the risen Lord reminded them again "that the Messiah must suffer and rise from the dead on the third day" (Lk. 24:46). Then his last words to the eleven promised a new empowering. "See, I send down upon you the promise of my Father. Remain here in the city until you are clothed with power from on high" (Lk. 24:49).

The early Christians recognized this power as God's own Spirit. When these final words of Jesus are repeated in the first chapter of Acts, the Holy Spirit is mentioned explicitly rather than the power from on high. "Wait, rather, for the fulfillment of my Father's promise, of which you have heard me speak. John baptized with water, but within a few days you will be baptized with the Holy Spirit" (Ac. 1:4f).

In response to this promise of the Holy Spirit, the apostles, still without understanding, asked about political power, wondering whether Jesus would restore Israel's rule once again (Ac 1:6). Jesus' response reiterated the promise of power, the new empowering by the Holy Spirit. "You will receive power when the Holy Spirit comes down on you; then you are to be my witnesses in Jerusalem, throughout Judea and Samaria, yes, even to the ends of the earth" (Ac. 1:8).

The entire Book of Acts testifies to the power of the Holy Spirit as the early Church continued the teaching and healing ministry of Jesus, and began to revolutionize the meaning of authority and power. Early in his preaching ministry, Peter addressed the question of power explicitly. After he and John had cured the crippled man at the Beautiful Gate of the temple, Peter asked the people, "Fellow Israelites, why does this surprise you? Why do you stare at us as if we had made this man walk by some power or holiness of our own?" (Ac. 3:12). He then spoke of the power of God at work in Jesus. "It is his name, and trust in this name, that has strengthened the limbs of this man whom you see and know well" (Ac. 3:16).

As a result of this cure and the subsequent proclamation of the power of Jesus, Peter and John were arrested. Again the question of power was raised, this time by the religious leaders. "By what power or in whose name have men of your stripe done this?" (Ac. 4:7). Peter, "filled with the Holy Spirit," answered their question directly, proclaiming the resurrection of Jesus whom they had crucified. "In the power of that name this man stands before you perfectly sound" (Ac. 4:8,10). The power of Jesus and the Holy Spirit, clearly at work in Peter, in John, and in the cured cripple amazed and threatened those leaders. How telling their remarks, "Everyone who lives in Jerusalem knows what a remarkable show of power took place through them. We cannot deny it" (Ac. 4:16).

This new empowerment in Jesus' own Holy Spirit enabled the disciples of Jesus to continue the mission of Jesus in fearless, courageous love. The last supper discourse in the Gospel of John gives some indication of the Holy Spirit's empowering role as comforter, advocate, and Spirit of truth (Jn. 14:17,26; 15:26; 16:13). That same discourse speaks of peace as Jesus' farewell gift (Jn. 14:27). This farewell gift of peace is intrinsically related to Jesus' farewell promise of the power from on high, the Holy Spirit.

Gradually the early Christians realized only the Spirit of God's own love as experienced in Jesus can enable any followers of Jesus to receive his gift of peace and thereby live as peacemakers in the sharing of that gift. Those early Christians witnessed to Jesus' way of love and peace in stark contrast to the ways of abusive, oppressive power and violence of any kind. Those early Christians were transformed by the Holy Spirit into persons of healing and forgiving love, persons of peacemaking ways, persons inaugurating a whole new way of community life, regardless of the opposition and suffering they encountered. Stephen's martyrdom account testifies admirably to this transforming power of the Holy Spirit (Ac. 7). That Christians of every age and culture would be so empowered is the reason for the missionary thrust of the Church pictured so graphically in Acts.

One of the early Christians' most striking statements on power is found in Paul's First Letter to the Corinthians. Referring to Christ crucified, Paul proclaimed, ". . . to those who are called, Jews and Greeks alike, Christ the power of God and the wisdom of God. For God's folly is wiser than men, and his weakness more powerful than men" (1Cor. 1:24f.).

Paul's relating power to wisdom is one more way to recognize that the empowerment of God in Christ and in Christians is an empowerment for a new way of life, one guided and directed by the wisdom of God. The challenge continues for each generation of Christians to receive God's empowering Spirit and thereby witness to the wise ways of the God of peace. Translating Jesus' peacemaking ways into political structures is a complex task in any period of history, but not an impossible one. The social teaching of the Church has pointed in that direction with increasing urgency. Commenting on the critical need for new political structures designed for peaceful solutions to the world's conflicts, *The Challenge of Peace* asserts the need for wisdom.

> In the nuclear age, it is in the regulation of interstate conflicts and ultimately the replacement of military by negotiated solutions that the supreme importance and necessity of a moral as well as a political concept of the international common good can be grasped. The absence of adequate structures for addressing these issues places even greater responsibility on the policies of individual states. By a mix of political vision and moral wisdom, states are called to interpret the national interest in light of the larger global interest (#243).

How well this statement resonates with the Gospel of Jesus

in its plea for the replacement of military power and its concern for global needs and international common good. Such global concern on the part of government calls for a radical conversion on the part of those possessing power and authority in the political sphere. A compassionate spirit for all the peoples of the world, especially those in most dire circumstances, and a spirit of forgiveness among nations must also play a dominant role in the restructuring of the world community if peace on earth is to become a reality.

In its urgent recommendations for new societal structures capable of making peace in a nuclear age, the peace pastoral also reminds us that the wisdom and power of God, desperately needed at this moment of human history, cannot be had without prayer. In prayer, ". . . we seek the wisdom to begin the search for peace and the courage to sustain us as instruments of Christ's peace in the world" (#293). In the light of this strong injunction, let us now turn our attention to a consideration of the relation of prayer to peacemaking.

Footnotes

[1] William Klassen, *Love of Enemies* (Philadelphia: Fortress Press 1984) p. 95.

[2] Hans Conzelmann, *The Theology of St. Luke*, tr. Geoffrey Buswell (New York: Harper and Row 1961) p. 75f. The entire first section of Conzelmann's classic Lucan study concentrates on the geographical elements of Lucan theology.

[3] Klassen, *Love*, p. 81f.

[4] John T. Pawlikowski and Donald Senior, eds., *Biblical and Theological Reflections on The Challenge of Peace* (Wilmington: Michael Glazier 1984) p. 81. A somewhat similar opinion is given in Albert Nolan's *Jesus before Christianity* (Maryknoll: Orbis 1978), ch. 14, "The Incident in the Temple." In the following chapter Nolan claims Jesus was not a pacifist in principle, but a pacifist in practice. I find great difficulty in understanding Nolan's position, and more difficulty in agreeing with it.

[5] Pawlikowski, *Biblical*, p. 81.

[6] Klassen, *Love*, p. 101.

[7] Augustine, *Against the Letters of Petilianus*, as quoted in Louis J. Swift, *The Early Fathers on War and Military Service* (Wilmington: Michael Glazier 1983) p. 147.

⁸ C. John Cadoux, *The Early Christian Attitude to War* (New York: Seabury Press 1982 reprint of 1919 edition) p. 34f.

⁹ Cf. Peter E. Fink, "Living the Sacrifice of Christ," *Worship* 59/2 (1985) p. 140. Fink refers to Metz's claim that the desert struggle is paradigmatic of all the choices Jesus made in his life.

¹⁰ Tertullian, *On Idolatry*, as quoted in Swift, *The Early*, p. 41f.

¹¹ Cf. Dianne Bergant, "Peace in a Universe of Order," in Pawlikowski and Senior, *Biblical*, pp. 17-30. The entire essay gives helpful insight into the problem of a warrior god interpretation of the Hebrew scriptures. Also see Bergant's article, "Yahweh: A Warrior God?" in *The Bible Today* 21:3 (1983).

¹² J. Carter Swaim, *War, Peace and the Bible* (Maryknoll: Orbis 1982). The entire book is pertinent, especially chapters 1, 2 and 3 with reference to the Hebrew scriptures.

¹³ Cadoux, *The Early*, p. 78f. Also see R. H. Bainton, *Christian Attitudes Toward War and Peace. A Historical Survey and Critical Evaluation* (New York: Abingdon Press 1960) p. 77.

¹⁴ Cf. Louis Swift, *The Early*, for an excellent survey of patristic opinion on peace and peacemaking. The book also includes patristic writings on war.

3.   Prayer of Peacemakers

The passion narratives in the four Gospels testify to the centrality of prayer in the life of Jesus. Those same passion narratives have offered Christians a contemplative experience which has been a source of strength and compassionate love for people in all walks of life. Today's challenge of peacemaking invites Christians to enter ever more fully into the prayer life of Jesus, particularly as known in the passion experience, and find therein the power and wisdom for making peace.

Jesus' life of prayer was formed through his Jewish faith life, guided by the Hebrew scriptures. In similiar fashion, the prayer life of the earliest Christians depended to a large extent on the prayer experiences they had known in Judaism. Consequently, it should not be surprising to find so many references to the Hebrew scriptures interwoven throughout the Gospels, including the passion narratives.

In a recent article, "The Passion According to Mark," Raymond Brown gives references to Isaiah's suffering servant of the Lord which are very significant in understanding the theology of Mark's passion narrative.[1] In the four Isaian servant songs, now incorporated into the Holy Week liturgy, not only do we find great insight into Jesus' own comprehension of the meaning of his life and death, we also find a theology of prayer which can be exceedingly life-giving for today's Christians called to be peacemakers.[2]

In pursuing the prayer theology of the servant songs, it is

important to appreciate the continuity present in all four songs (Is. 42:1-9; 49:1-6; 50:4-9; 52:13-53:12).[3] In some ways, these songs could be compared to four movements of a symphony. In order to receive the full import of such a musical composition, one must listen to all the movements. Any segment of a symphony or other artistic work considered in isolation from the whole composition makes full enjoyment of that artistic creation impossible.

In the Isaian servant songs, the themes presented in the first song influence the theology of the other songs. So too, does the theology of the second song influence the third and fourth songs, and so on. Awareness of this continuity factor is particularly important in the consideration of the theology of prayer, presented as it is in the context of the whole life experience of the servant.

The first servant song (42:1-9) introduces this profound theology with Yahweh pointing to the servant as "my chosen one." Before commenting on any of Yahweh's words, the significance of Yahweh's initiative in the ongoing relationship between Yahweh and the servant must be highlighted. Servant theology cannot be separated from covenant theology. Both servant and covenant speak to the mystery of friendship with God, a mystery of intimate love so amazing that denial of the possibility of such a relationship sometimes seems a more logical option than accepting the offer of friendship on God's terms.

Genuine friendship is never a one-sided affair. Someone must take initiative in beginning a friendship; the other person must respond freely. Without such freedom of initiative and freedom of response, a friendship cannot even begin to exist.

Every aspect of the friendship God desires with the chosen servant depends on the initiative of God's love. At first sight, our English word "servant," suggesting images of household maids and butlers, is not a very precise translation of the Hebrew *ebed*, the word for servant. Even certain political uses of the word, such as public servant, do not begin to capture the meaning of *ebed Yahweh*. The suffering servant of Yahweh is a special friend of God, one who does serve Yahweh's people, but in ways exalted far beyond the ordinary ways service is rendered by one person to another.

Friendship always necessitates dialog, the kind of dialog which depends on a listening in love. When one of the friends is God, then the dialog initiating, sustaining, and enlivening the friendship is prayer. The Isaian servant songs witness to such dialog. At times Yahweh is the singer; at other times, the servant sings.

In identifying "my servant whom I uphold, my chosen one with whom I am pleased" (42:1), Yahweh initiates a relationship which inaugurates a life of prayer. Before considering further implications of prayer in the context of the servant's mission, the Gospel use of this servant text deserves comment.

Each of the synoptic writers inserts a reworking of this Isaian servant text into the accounts of Jesus' baptism (Mt. 3:17; Mk. 1:11; Lk. 3:22). Such use of this servant text from the Hebrew scriptures serves to identify Jesus as Yahweh's servant as he prepares to inaugurate his public ministry. In this light, the servant theology helps explain all of Jesus' ministry, culminating in his passion and death. The servant theology also gives helpful insight into Jesus' developing life of prayer.

God's initiative in establishing a friendship with the chosen servant includes the gift of God's own spirit. Without this gift of Yahweh's spirit, the sharing of life which this new friendship entails would not be possible. The reasons for the spirit's empowering are almost overwhelming. Nothing less than bringing justice to all the nations is envisioned as Yahweh expounds this servant song: "Upon whom I have put my spirit; he (the servant) shall bring forth justice to the nations" (42:1).

Three times in this first servant song the issue of justice is sounded. Verse 6 identifies the vocation of the servant with the call to justice. "I, the Lord, have called you for the victory of justice." Verse 4 promises that the servant's efforts for justice will persevere to the end. The servant will continue in his mission "until he establishes justice on the earth; the coastlands will wait for his teaching."

Perhaps no one has clarified more carefully the biblical meaning of justice than John R. Donahue in his essay, "Biblical Perspectives on Justice." Drawing on contemporary scripture scholarship, both Catholic and Protestant, Donahue explains justice as "fidelity to the demands of a relationship."[4] Then this biblical understanding of justice is traced through the Hebrew scriptures, the intertestamental literature, and the New Testament. In concluding this study, Donahue emphasized that the bible is not interested in abstract notions of justice primarily. Rather, the bible treats justice as a matter of action to establish and maintain the kind of relationships which witness to covenant fidelity. "Peace and harmony are the fruits of justice as well as its signs."[5]

One of the ways peace is related to this strong justice theme in the servant theology is in the approach the servant will use to establish justice on earth. "A bruised reed he shall not break, and a smoldering wick he shall not quench" (42:3). The poetic imagery used here needs to be pondered. Establishing justice on the earth is a monumental task, one which would seem to call for ways and means of enormous strength and influence and power. Throughout history people have used violent means at times in their efforts to secure justice. Caring for a bruised reed and a smoldering wick hardly suggests the victory of justice reaching to the coastlands.

Anyone who has tried to save a bruised reed, whether it be a small garden plant trampled by a scampering rabbit, or a wheat field damaged by a ravaging storm, knows that only a careful handling and bracing of a bruised reed can help nurture the weakened life back to a condition of health. So too, with a smoldering wick of an oil lamp or candle. Only a gentle shifting of oil or wax and air can prevent the flame from total extinction and help rekindle the tiny fire. When these images of bruised reed and smoldering wick are translated in human terms, then the gentle healing touches are even more necessary. Bruised and broken persons need the careful touches of compassionate love for healing to take place.

These images of strong gentleness are startling in their context of a mission to bring justice to the nations. In contemporary terms, these images speak of nonviolence as a way to justice, and imply nonviolence as a way to peace. The placement of these images at the beginning of the first servant song should not be overlooked. Only because of the endowment with Yahweh's spirit is this different nonviolent approach possible. Empowered by Yahweh's spirit, the servant will use this approach of compassionate healing in all his ongoing efforts for justice and for peace. The many implications of this nonviolent way of bringing about justice and peace will unfold as the servant enters into his mission under the influence of Yahweh's spirit.

The role of Yahweh's spirit in the life of the servant is described in the context of a new creation theology. God, the Lord, who has chosen the servant is the same God "who created the heavens and stretched them out, who spreads out the earth with its crops, who gives breath to its people and spirit to those who walk on it" (42:5). This creator of the universe, having called the servant for the victory of justice, continues to sing of how the servant has been formed with God's own personal creative touch. "I have grasped you by the hand; I formed you, and set you as a covenant of the people, a light for the nations" (42:6).

This new creation theology, with its obvious reminders of the Yahwist creation account in Genesis (Gn. 2:4f), places the creative power of God in central focus. Immediately following the nonviolent imagery of bruised reed and smoldering wick, this reminder of God's power is highly significant because the servant is called to a mission of worldwide import. As will become increasingly clear, the servant's mission of establishing justice and peace demands a steady conviction of the never-failing power of God at work in the world God created. The servant's mission also demands the servant's unfaltering confidence in

God's creative love at work in the core of his own being as he undertakes the mission he was chosen to accomplish.

Describing the servant's mission as "covenant of the people and light for the nations" then focuses the creative power of God on forming a new covenant at the heart of the new creation. The Isaian servant songs are not unique in speaking of a new covenant. Jeremiah prophesied that a new covenant would be established, one characterized by intimacy with God. "But this is the covenant which I will make with the house of Israel after those days, says the Lord. I will place my law within them, and write it upon their hearts; I will be their God, and they shall be my people" (Je. 31:33).

When Ezechiel spoke of a new covenant, he too stressed great intimacy with God made possible by the gift of God's spirit. "I will give you a new heart and place a new spirit within you, taking from your bodies your stony hearts and giving you natural hearts. I will put my spirit within you and make you live by my statutes, careful to observe my decrees" (Ez. 36:25f). This new oneness with God, this new heart and new spirit would enable the people of God to live in covenant fidelity and would issue forth in a resurgence of prayerfulness. As a result, the right relationships of justice would prevail along with a new fulness of life and peace.

The Challenge of Peace refers explicitly to the covenantal proclamations of Jeremiah, Ezechiel, and Isaiah (#35). The obligations of justice, especially for the poor and needy, are presented as basic to covenant fidelity with its promise of peace (#34). Ezechiel is singled out as the prophet who made the covenantal relation to peace most explicit (#33).

However, in the first servant song there is another aspect of the new covenant which adds to the covenant promises of Ezechiel and Jeremiah. Yahweh sings of the servant as a covenant of the people. Somehow the servant will be instrumental in establishing the new relation of friendship between God and those who would be known as the people of God. Such a mission would necessitate an enjoyment of friendship first between

Yahweh and the servant. Only from the experience of this new covenant of friendship could this same covenant relation be extended further in any authentic way by the servant.

This covenant of the people is to be a light for the nations, one which will "open the eyes of the blind, bring out the prisoners from confinement and from the dungeon, those who live in darkness" (42:7). Here, in the context of the light for all the nations, Yahweh promises that a people covenanted to God in friendship has a universal influence, one which is characterized predominantly by light. Through this covenanted people, those blinded and held captive by injustices of any kind will see light and be freed from oppression.

There are many ways to interpret this covenant established through the servant's mission. In our time, when the Second Vatican Council keynoted its *Dogmatic Constitution on the Church* with the phrase, "light to all nations," the need for a contemporary hermeneutic of the servant songs was implied. This scriptural way of describing the people of God as servant identifies the church as a covenantal community of intimate union with God and thereby capable of sharing God's own ways of establishing justice and peace. This descriptive phrase of universal light applied to today's church must be understood in the context of the entire servant theology, including the life of prayer which the servant identity calls forth.

The final verses of this first servant song sound a message of undaunted hope because of the creative power of God. New things will "spring into being" (42:9) as the servant follows the lead of Yahweh's spirit in covenant fidelity and begins to establish justice on the earth.

Before considering the ongoing mission of the servant as proclaimed in the second servant song, Jesus' direct reference to the imagery of the first song should be noted. Luke gives us the Nazareth synagogue scene which follows the accounts of Jesus' baptism and desert struggle. In the Nazareth synagogue, Jesus read a servant passage from a later section of Isaiah.

"The Spirit of the Lord is upon me; therefore, he has anointed me. He has sent me to bring glad tidings to the poor, to proclaim liberty to captives, recovery of sight to the blind and release to prisoners, to announce a year of favor from the Lord" (Lk. 4:18f; Is. 61:1f).

Although this passage is not a direct quotation from one of the four servant songs in Second Isaiah, the themes of "healing the broken-hearted" and giving "liberty to captives" are similar. Most basic is the servant's anointing with the Lord's own spirit. When Jesus is pictured in this servant context as he begins his public ministry soon after his baptismal anointing with the Spirit, the Lucan author once again is highlighting servant theology as a key way of understanding Jesus. Early on in his Christology, Sobrino emphasizes the importance of recognizing how Jesus' life "took on the features of the work attributed to the suffering servant of Yahweh."[6]

The second servant song (49:1-6) is sung by the servant and begins with an acknowledged acceptance of Yahweh's call. Reminiscent of the way Jeremiah described the beginnings of his prophetic vocation (Je. 1:5), the servant proclaims even to distant peoples that "the Lord called me from birth, from my mother's womb he gave me my name" (49:1).

This freely given response to Yahweh's call is an essential factor in the life of intimate friendship which Yahweh offered the servant. Hardly any human imagery could speak of greater intimacy than that of a child in its mother's womb. It's almost as if the servant is singing of Yahweh's predilection as being a bit impatient. Yahweh couldn't wait for the servant to be born. From the beginning of the servant's existence, God was calling and naming the servant as covenant of the people and light for the nations.

The dialogical pattern evident in this second song is instructive insofar as it witnesses to a communing process inherent in a love relationship. In a somewhat imperceptible way this communing pattern introduces the theme of prayer which begins to be described in more explicit imagery as the song progresses.

In rather sharp contrast to the first servant song's images of bruised reed and smoldering wick, the second song sings of a sharp-edged sword and a polished arrow. "He made of me a sharp-edged sword and concealed me in the shadow of his arm. He made me a polished arrow, in his quiver he hid me" (49:2). Through military imagery the servant's mission is described in ways which help identify the servant as a prophet, one who speaks Yahweh's words of life-giving love for the people whose life he shares.

The renowned biblical scholar, Gerhard Von Rad, has been particularly helpful in describing the servant in the context of one who is gifted with a prophetic vocation.[7] The servant is really the prophet *par excellence*, one whose life speaks not only in accord with his words, but more loudly and persuasively than any words ever could. This prophetic motif continues in the third and fourth songs and is dependent on the prayerfulness of the servant.

At first sight, a sharp-edged sword and a polished arrow may seem to have little to do with a prophet, much less with prayer. Like the bruised reed and smoldering wick, this imagery must be pondered carefully. The text makes it clear that the sword and arrow are ways of describing the prophet servant. Such transformation of military imagery is not to be interpreted in some text-proof fashion as a polemic for military activity and warmaking. Unfortunately, similar scriptural references to military practices have been misused to justify warmaking on the part of Christians.[8] Quite the contrary interpretation is intended, a point which the peace pastoral addressed (#41). The scriptural transformation of military imagery is precisely that — a transformation. Whenever it occurs in scripture, transformed military imagery can be instrumental in helping the people of God move from a stance culturally conditioned by centuries of warmaking, to a transformed position of peacemaking. The transformed sharp-edged sword and polished arrow of the servant songs is a classic case in point.

A strange thing happens to both the sword and the arrow. Both are concealed or hidden by Yahweh. The sword is concealed in the shadow of Yahweh's arm; the arrow is hidden in Yahweh's quiver. Obviously these descriptions speak in anthropomorphic terms, giving Yahweh a human body with arms and hands to hold a sword, and a hip on which to brace a quiver of arrows. What may seem surprising at first is the suggestion of prayer in this transformed military imagery.

In order to understand the prayerfulness implied here, one must first face the implications of describing the prophet servant as a sharp-edged sword and a polished arrow. When a prophet functions as a sharp-edged sword, the prophet's words cut through the ambiguities, confusions, and frequent half-truths of a situation. The prophet speaks God's word of truth in unmistakably clear ways. Clarifying issues and bringing forth true facts in situations crying out for freedom from injustice and oppression is a necessary part of peacemaking. This is one way to describe the prophet servant's mission to bring light to the nations. In contemporary times, perhaps no one has been more convinced than Gandhi of the power of truth in the ongoing struggle for justice and peace. Unfaltering confidence in the power of truth is a basic philosophical tenet of Gandhian nonviolence.[9]

When the prophet servant is described as a polished arrow, then a slightly different aspect of his truth-giving message is emphasized. Skilled archers are trained to hit targets with precision. In applying such imagery to a prophetic word, the focus is on the ability to speak to the heart of an issue, to get right to the point which really makes the crucial difference in a situation. Furthermore, arrows have a singular way of penetrating deeply. In this context, the prophetic word reaches into the heart of a person, the very center of one's entire being. Such imagery implies that the prophetic word of truth is spoken in genuine love.

The ability to speak the truth in love, a manner of action characteristic of Yahweh's prophet servant, depends on the life of friendship with Yahweh continually nourished by prayer. This prayerfulness is included in surprising ways in the sword and arrow imagery. When applied to a prophet, a sword concealed in the shadow of Yahweh's arm and an arrow hidden in Yahweh's quiver can suggest a posture of resting close to the heart of God. This kind of resting implies a maturing prayerfulness. As in any friendship, it takes time to be comfortable in one another's presence with a quietness which bespeaks a joy in just being together. When this experience of friendship is understood in the context of prayer, then a traditional description such as 'prayer of quiet' can be helpful in designating a life of prayer which is developing and maturing.

In the life of the prophet servant this maturing prayer life is essential to the prophetic mission. The word spoken cannot be Yahweh's word, unless the prophet rests in God from time to time in order to hear the word authentically. The somewhat surprising and puzzling imagery of the concealed sword and hidden arrow can speak to this pattern of prayerful resting in God.

Before commenting on the servant's reporting of his prayerful dialog with Yahweh, one further point must be noted with respect to the military imagery inserted in this second servant song. Does such imagery promote the notion of a warrior God? This serious question of warrior god imagery was treated briefly in *The Challenge of Peace* and represents a pastoral concern which is crucial to peacemaking attitudes and actions.

After commenting on the "multifaceted connotations" of Israel's warrior god metaphor, the peace pastoral points to the gradual transformation of this image in the Hebrew scriptures, particularly after the exile (#31). The pastoral letter then elaborates somewhat on the meaning of the covenant relation as a major factor in offsetting the warrior god image. In the brief New Testament section, the pastoral states emphatically that in the Christian scriptures "there is no notion of a warrior God who will lead the people in an historical victory over its enemies" (#40).

Warrior gods are very compatible with punishing gods. These false gods wreak havoc with a life of prayer because they make a life of friendship with God impossible. Later in this study, some consideration will be given to historical examples in which the image of a punishing, vengeful god helped justify violence on the part of Christians. But in the present treatment of prayer and peacemaking as exemplified in the servant theology, what cannot be overlooked is the essential relation between one's perception of God as influenced or controlled by key images, and one's ability to mature in the kind of prayer life necessary for a peacemaker.

A valuable contribution to this discussion of one's perception of God is made by Gordon Zahn in an essay entitled, "Pacifism and the Just War." In his remarks on the spirituality of pacifism, Zahn rightly claims that accurate perceptions of God are crucial to a peacemaker's commitment and behavior. After commenting on the incompatibility of a vindictive god with the peacemaker's perception of an omnipotent, benign creator, infinitely willing to forgive, Zahn states how impossible it is for a person seriously committed to the cause of peace to reconcile and to be animated by the all-too-prevalent popular notion of a vengeful god.[10]

One simple conclusion to be drawn from this brief consideration of the devastating effects of a warrior, vengeful, punishing god image is to do everything possible, in the pastoral order, to replace such images with the image of the God of Jesus, an image definitely influenced by the God of Isaian servant theology. It cannot be overemphasized that one's perception of God is most basic to peacemaking because one's perception of God determines how one's prayer life will develop. The servant of Yahweh testifies to a very different God than one who is vengefully plotting punishing devices, including wars. The God of the servant of Yahweh, like the God of Jesus, is a God of compassion, a God entrusting the ways of peace to a covenanted people who are guided continually by that God's own spirit.

In all of the servant songs, perhaps no part witnesses more

convincingly to a compassionate God than the verses in the
second song immediately following the description of the
prophet servant as a sword and an arrow resting in God. This
God promises to show divine glory, no less, through the servant.
Furthermore, the servant sometimes takes on the communal
identity of the whole of Israel, that covenanted people made so
through the servant's mission. "You are my servant, he said to
me, Israel, through whom I show my glory" (49:3).

Then, when the servant discloses in unreserved honesty the
tiredness, exhaustion, and discouragement which have
mounted in his life because of the demands of his mission, God
not only becomes more than ever the servant's strength, but
also wards off any disheartened feelings with exciting words
of promise. "It is too little, he says, for you to be my servant,
to raise up the tribes of Jacob, and restore the survivors of
Israel; I will make you a light to the nations, that my salvation
may reach to the ends of the earth" (49:6).

It is imperative that the prophet servant be reminded that
his influence extends far beyond the immediate time and place
of the servant's action. Largely because of the servant's prayerfulness, constantly strengthening the oneness with God characteristic of the covenant relation, the impact of the prophet servant's message will be extended in ways only the creator God
can envision. In these final verses of the second servant song,
the creator God is also a saving God whose salvation will reach
to the ends of the earth because of the mysterious ways
Yahweh's prophet servant will be light to the nations.

The third servant song (50:4-9) serves as a bridge between
the prophet servant's life of active ministry and life of suffering.
This song is also most explicit about the centrality of prayer
in the servant's life.

As the servant begins to sing of his mission, he is most explicit
in identifying his role as prophet. "The Lord God has given me
a well-trained tongue, that I might know how to speak to the
weary a word that will rouse them" (50:4). Reference to the
weary in this song resonates with the bruised reed and smolder-

ing wick of the first song. Both images speak to the oppressed poor of the world, those countless persons who are hurt, broken, and exhausted because of mounting injustices in their lives. Both images speak to nonviolent action, but in different ways. In this song, the prophet's words inspire and rouse the weary people with confidence and hope in God's compassionate love empowering them in their struggle for justice. To comprehend something of the profound truth in this description of prophetic action, one has only to recall, in contemporary times, the poor peoples' response to the prophetic words of nonviolent leaders such as Mahatma Gandhi, Martin Luther King, Jr., and Cesar Chavez. Even more telling are the Gospel descriptions of the crowds listening to the life-giving words of Jesus.

This third song also relates directly to the second song in its strong emphasis on prayer as the source of the inspiring power of the prophet servant's words. Morning after morning Yahweh opens the ear of the prophet servant that he may hear (50:4). This description of a continual listening stance is a favored way of describing prayer in the religious heritage of Jesus. For the fervent Jew, first and foremost prayer is a listening to God. When that listening is characterized as a constant attentiveness, a "morning after morning" listening, then the prayerfulness under consideration has matured to a state of continual oneness.[11] That kind of listening in faithful love is at the heart of the prophet servant's life. Without such prayerfulness the prophet's words would be "noisy gong and clanging cymbal" (1Cor. 13:1). With such a life of faithful prayer, the prophet servant's words would ring true as the word of God. With the empowering strength possible only through a mature prayer life, the prophet servant could withstand the suffering bound to enter his life sooner or later.

The suffering motif enters almost abruptly in the third servant song. Immediately after the prophet servant sings of the wonders of God's faithful communing in prayer, we hear: "And I have not rebelled, have not turned back. I gave my back to those who beat me, my cheeks to those who plucked my beard;

my face I did not shield from buffets and spitting" (50:5f). These descriptions of violent cruelty are startling; the servant's lack of retaliation, even more so. Resistance to the prophet servant's message has provoked unbridled opposition, even personal attack. In response the servant sings of the strengthening power of God who reassures the servant of his own integrity. "The Lord God is my help (50:7,9), therefore I am not disgraced; I have set my face like flint, knowing that I shall not be put to shame" (50:7).

As the third servant song moves into the fourth (52:13-53:12), the servant becomes the suffering servant of Yahweh. Significantly, the fourth song begins with Yahweh extending an invitation to contemplation, posing the simple word, "See." For those who accept this invitation, what is there to see? Yahweh's chosen servant, "raised high and greatly exalted" (52:13); an appearance marred "beyond that of mortals" (52:14); "no stately bearing to make us look at him" (53.2); "a man of suffering, accustomed to infirmity" (53.3).

As the song continues, those who enter this contemplative experience question why the servant endures such suffering. This question and its mysterious answer are somewhat reminiscent of the story of Job. In the servant's sufferings, sufferings which crush him for the sins of his people, those same people are made whole (53:5). Even more mysterious is the fact that "the Lord laid upon him the guilt of us all" (53:6) and was even "pleased to crush him in infirmity" (53:10). This servant "had done no wrong nor spoken any falsehood" (53:9). "Though he was harshly treated, he submitted and opened not his mouth" (53:7). In all this mysterious suffering "the will of the Lord shall be accomplished through him" (53:10).

In the final verses of the song, once again Yahweh is the singer, promising that the servant "shall see the light in fullness of days; through this suffering, my servant shall justify many, and their guilt he shall bear" (53:11). As the song concludes, the servant is promised "a portion among the great," and a division of "the spoils with the mighty" (53:12). All these signs of exaltation will be accomplished "because he surrendered himself to death and was counted among the wicked" (53:12). Finally, Yahweh proclaims that the servant "shall take away the sins of many, and win pardon for their offenses" (53:12). *The Jerusalem Bible* translates this final phrase, "he was bearing the faults of many and praying all the time for sinners."

The invitation to contemplate this servant song has been accepted by countless people of faith, both Jewish and Christian, scholars and others, down through the centuries. For the earliest Christians, including the Gospel writers, this fourth servant song provided a most helpful way to begin to comprehend some meaning in the passion and death of Jesus. In the entire bible there is hardly a comparable passage which speaks more clearly to the compassionate love of God entering into and transforming human suffering caused by human sin. Perhaps the most profound part of this mystery is the way in which God empowers a human person, the servant, to make God's compassionate love visible. In a unique way, God's glory is shown through the servant (49:3).

In his commentary on *Second Isaiah*, Carroll Stuhlmueller stresses the great solidarity the suffering servant shared with the people of God.[12] Whatever else might be said about the servant of Yahweh, this person knew by experience the agony and anguish of a suffering people. With a love which could be explained only by an extraordinary union with God, the servant entered into his people's sufferings caused by their infidelity to the covenant. Accepting suffering rather than inflicting it, the servant won pardon for the people and "justified many" (53:11). The servant did bring about the victory of justice and made the way clear for peace.

Whenever meaning is found in the servant songs, the contemplation required includes some experiential awareness born of suffering in love. This contemplative attitude climaxes the life of prayer characteristic of one anointed with God's own spirit. No one lived the servant life more devotedly than Jesus, whose prayer on the cross testified to his fidelity even through the suffering of abandonment.

Today, as already noted, the Second Vatican Council has called the entire church to become a servant church as disciples of Jesus. Vatican II projected a church strong enough to enter into the modern world's joys and hopes, griefs and anxieties, and transform those situations which are responsible for untold suffering.[13] In today's world, not just crying out but screaming in pain under the scourge of war, a world starving more and more of its poor through an arms race preparing for global crucifixion,[14] nothing is more crucial for persons of faith than following the way of Yahweh's servant. This way is a way of mature prayer enabling both persons and communities to enter more completely into the mystery of God's compassionate love. This way of Yahweh's servant promises the victory of justice along with the forgiveness and pardon which make for peace.

Footnotes

[1] Raymond E. Brown, "The Passion According to Mark," *Worship* 59/2 (1985) pp. 120,122.

[2] A condensed version of the material presented in this chapter can be found in the *Pax Christi International Bulletin* (Antwerp: Pax Christi International 1986). Included is a report of the first International Pax Christi Retreat, held in the St. Catherine Labouré Retreat Center, Fain les Moutiers, France, in August, 1984. During the retreat I presented two conferences on the servant songs.

[3] Scholars do not agree on the precise verses of all of the servant songs. I have followed John L. McKenzie's designation except for the first song. Strictly speaking, the song ends with verse 4. Verses 5-9 explicate the servant's mission and are helpful in understanding the servant theology in its entirety. Cf. John L. McKenzie, *Second Isaiah, The Anchor Bible* (Garden City: Doubleday 1968) p. xxxviii f.

[4] John R. Donahue, "Biblical Perspectives on Justice," in John C. Haughey, ed., *The Faith That Does Justice* (New York: Paulist 1977) p. 69.

[5] Donahue, "Biblical," p. 108.

[6] Jon Sobrino, *Christology at the Crossroads*, tr. John Drury (Maryknoll: Orbis 1978) p. 58.

[7] Gerhard Von Rad, *The Message of the Prophets*, tr. D.M.G. Stalker (New York: Harper & Row 1965) p. 218f.

[8] Louis J. Swift, *The Early Fathers on War and Military Service* (Wilmington: Michael Glazier 1983) p. 19.

[9] Cf. Ignatius Jesudasan, *A Gandhian Theology of Liberation* (Maryknoll: Orbis 1984) p. 93f.

[10] Gordon Zahn, "Pacifism and the Just War," in Philip J. Murnion, ed., *Catholics and Nuclear War* (New York: Crossroad 1983) p. 121f.

[11] Von Rad, *The Message*, p. 221.

[12] Carroll Stuhlmueller, "Deutero-Isaiah" in *The Jerome Biblical Commentary* (Englewood Cliffs: Prentice-Hall 1968) p. 366f.

[13] Vatican II's *Pastoral Constitution on the Church* begins with the statement: *"The joys and hopes, the griefs and the anxieties of the men of this age, especially those who are poor or in any way afflicted, these too are the joys and hopes, the griefs and anxieties of the followers of Christ. Indeed, nothing genuinely human fails to raise an echo in their hearts."* Walter Abbott, ed., *The Documents of Vatican II* (New York: Guild Press, America Press, Association Press 1966) p. 199f.

[14] Archbishop Hunthausen of Seattle has used crucifixion imagery to describe the nuclear madness of our times. In his own words: "Our nuclear war preparations are the global crucifixion of Jesus. What we do to the least of these, through our nuclear war planning, we do to Jesus. This is his teaching. We cannot avoid it and we should not try. Our nuclear weapons are the final crucifixion of Jesus, the extermination of the human family with whom he is one." Quoted in "A Pilgrim's Journal: Daily Lenten Reflections for Peacemakers," compiled by Pax Christi USA (Erie, PA 1985).

4 Playfulness and Peacemaking

"Playfulness and Peacemaking" might seem like a surprising title on two accounts. First of all, when one tries to confront the horrible potential of today's nuclear arsenals, or even the pitiable condition of one wounded war veteran, playfulness seems an inappropriate and totally irrelevant response, to say the least. Secondly, associating play with the Gospel passion narratives seems equally incongruous, unless one wants to recall the soldiers throwing dice for Jesus' garments as a bizarre example of play (Jn. 19:24).

But the passion story is hopelessly incomplete without the resurrection accounts. Conversely, there is no meaning in the resurrection of Jesus without his passion and death experience. Commentaries on the Gospel stories of the risen Jesus wrestle with many important questions, such as the difficulties in harmonizing the four accounts, the meaning of the empty tomb, and the actual bodily resurrection of Jesus.[1] Rarely, if ever, is any consideration given to the quality of playfulness which emerges in the resurrection stories. For that matter, play and playfulness have received very little attention in theological writings.[2]

This sad lack of a viable theology of play may have much to do with an inability on the part of so many Christians to become peacemakers. However, before we look at the correlation between playfulness and peacemaking in Christian life, a word must be said about playfulness itself. Then the question of playfulness in the resurrection stories can be probed as prelude to the consideration of playfulness and peacemaking today.

Play and playfulness of their very nature almost defy definition. Descriptions are much more in order than definitions when one ponders the phenomenon of play. Naming characteristics common to playfulness also helps one grasp some meaning in this delightful human activity called play.

A few contemporary theologians have made valuable contributions to the development of a theology of play. Early on in his insightful book, *In Praise of Play, Toward a Psychology of Religion*, Robert Neale gives a somewhat negative definition of play. "Play is psychologically defined as *any activity not motivated by the need to resolve inner conflict.*"[3] Neale elaborates on the inner harmony which a genuinely playful person possesses when two basic needs are reconciled: the need to discharge energy and the need to design experience.[4] A religious person is filled with this inner harmony and therefore experiences great inner peace and freedom — a "player's piety."[5]

As Neale develops his theory of a player's piety, he emphasizes that a playful person is not concerned about resolving inner conflict and consequently is free to respond to the needs of others, even to the point of suffering. Neale asserts, "Only the player is capable of love."[6]

In *Man at Play*, Hugo Rahner, writing as an historian of religion, gives a delightful theological perspective on the playing of God as the reason underlying all the playing of human persons. Human playfulness culminating in a heavenly dance is possible because the creator God is a playing God whose creatures are made in this Creator's image and likeness and therefore must play. Rahner claims, "There is a sacral secret at the root and in the flowering of all play: it is man's hope for another life taking visible form in gesture . . . Man at play is reaching out for that superlative ease, in which even the body, freed from its earthly burden, moves to the effortless measures of a heavenly dance."[7] Like Neale, Rahner elaborates on the inner harmony which all human play presupposes and expresses.[8]

Characteristics of God's playfulness are cited by Walter Ong in his preface to Rahner's treatise. Ong states that because God's work is always joyous, spontaneous, and completely free, the work of God is always play.[9] These characteristics of joy, spontaneity, and freedom are key in understanding genuine playfulness, whether it be the playfulness of God or the playfulness of the children of God.

Drawing on the wisdom of early Greek philosophers along with the faith vision of Greek and Latin patristic writers who highlighted the playfulness of the divine,[10] Rahner focuses on the creative play of God as it is reflected in the creative play of God's children. Spontaneity and freedom are intrinsic to God's creative play. The creative process is entered into with utmost freedom, because it is a work (or a play) of totally selfless love. Commenting on both creation and incarnation as expressions of divine love, Rahner also reminds us that such unfathomable mysteries can be named only in a negative theology. Paul attempted to theologize in this negative manner when he spoke of God's foolishness and weakness, characteristics of children.[11]

Surprise is another characteristic of play, both human and divine. Neale goes so far as to say that the Holy might even be defined as the Surprising. If creation does not provide ample evidence for a surprising, playful God, then "the story of the Word become flesh and the game of Communion which celebrates it" testify unmistakably to a surprising God.[12]

Joy, freedom, spontaneity, and surprise are perhaps most evident and observable whenever children play. A child's imaginings create wonderful surprises in piles of sand or clay, with building blocks and erector sets, with bits and pieces of almost anything freely fashioning a play house or a play school or a play store. Was this joyful ability to imagine and create something new one of the reasons why Jesus told his disciples that they must become as little children in order to enter the kingdom (Mt. 18:1f)?[13] Jesus also rejoiced in the Holy Spirit and praised his Father as Lord of heaven and earth because of all God had revealed to the merest children (Lk. 10:21).

In discussing the playing of God, Rahner relates two striking passages from different historical periods which associate the playfulness of a child with the eternal Logos who is also Son of God. Gregory Nazianzen spoke in these Christological terms when he described the freedom and ingenuity of the creative process in terms of playfulness.

> For the Logos on high plays,
> stirring the whole cosmos back and forth, as he wills
> into shapes of every kind.[14]

Closer to our own day, Cornelius a Lapide expressed the relationship of Son to Father in trinitarian life as an eternal game of a child. "The Son is called a child because of his proceeding everlasting from the Father, because in the dewy freshness and springtime beauty of his eternal youth he eternally enacts a game before his Father."[15]

In our own times, Christological developments enable us to see the playfulness of Son and Logos not only in the context of a creation theology, but also in terms of the resurrection of Jesus as the culmination of his life of complete fidelity to his Father. Jon Sobrino stresses the importance of emphasizing the relational aspect of Jesus' human life, because the category of relationship enables us to appreciate in some ways the evolutionary dynamic in Jesus' own sonship. Once we begin to understand that Jesus' relation to the Father is really the history of that relationship, then we can speak of the human Jesus becoming the Son.[16] That is to say, as Jesus truly grew in wisdom, age, grace, and faith; as Jesus lived and suffered and died in faithfulness, his relationship to his Father expressed ever more completely the reality of Son, of child of God in the most beautiful way possible. Therefore, in risen life, Jesus will add new joy and freedom and spontaneity and surprise to the playfulness he possesses eternally as Logos.

The New Testament accounts of the appearances of the risen Jesus give many indications of Jesus' playfulness. Surprise, joy, freedom, and spontaneity, those common characteristics of play, are found throughout the stories of Jesus' meetings with his friends and disciples.

Before considering examples which illustrate this playful spirit of Jesus, it might be helpful to comment on the way the risen Jesus addressed his disciples on that early morning at daybreak after they had been fishing all through the night. "He said to them, 'Children, have you caught anything to eat?'" (Jn. 21:5). Of the many ways Jesus might have called out to them, his use of the word "children" does seem a bit surprising. They were robust fishermen, even though they had caught nothing that particular night. At the Last Supper, Jesus did not hesitate to call them friends and he told them why. "I have made known to you all that I heard from my Father (Jn. 15:15). But now, these soon-to-be leaders of the first Christian communities were called children.

To appreciate the playful innuendos in this timely designation, children, it is necessary to recall the entire scene. Jesus was preparing a lakeside picnic, replete with charcoal cooked food. If such a simple description seems inappropriate, perhaps a child's imagination can be helpful in grasping the meaning of this event. I remember a fourth grade teacher sharing the drawing of one of her students. That young boy had depicted this Gospel scene with Jesus standing over a modern charcoal grill cooking the fish. All the joviality of a picnic came through in the drawing.

In addition to the picnic atmosphere of that lakeside morning, the disciples were surprised in utter amazement at the number of fish they had caught after they followed Jesus' suggestion. One hundred fifty-three fish is hardly a small catch, especially if laboring for an entire night had netted not so much as a single fish. But most of all, they were surprised by Jesus' appearing in that early dawning hour. They were not expecting him then and there. They finally recognized him through his actions, but not at first, by his calling them "children." Was this title merely a way to help them relax and move into the playful spirit of a picnic, or was something more pertinent also intended by Jesus?

In the Johannine Gospel two previous appearances of the risen Jesus to his disciples are recorded (Jn. 20:19f and 26f). On both occasions Jesus' greeting was "Peace be with you." In the first appearance he repeated the greeting after showing his disciples his wounded hands and side to help them believe he was the same Jesus who had suffered and died and was now risen. In Matthew's Gospel, when Mary Magdalen and the other Mary were hurrying away from the empty tomb to tell the disciples the surprising good news of the resurrection, "Suddenly, without warning, Jesus stood before them and said, 'Peace!'" (Mt. 28:9). Luke reports the same greeting of "Peace to you" as Jesus surprised his disciples on the way to Emmaus (Lk. 24:36). Without a doubt, "Peace" was the characteristic greeting of the risen Jesus. But when we come to this episode by the sea of Galilee, the greeting shifts from "Peace" to "Children."

If there is a significant relationship between these greetings of "Peace" and "Children," then some understanding of peace in Jesus' Hebraic heritage must be reflected on prior to the consideration of a possible relation between these salutations of the risen Jesus.[17] *The Challenge of Peace* gives a brief indication of some of the various aspects of peace as found in the Hebrew scriptures (#32). After emphasizing that "all notions of peace must be understood in light of Israel's relation to God," the pastoral notes that peace is a gift from God, resulting from God's saving activity. From the Hebrew point of view, it is a misconception to think of peace in terms of an individual's personal well-being and wholeness as predominant over the unity and harmony of the community. Furthermore, a right ordering of all creation is included in the meaning of *shalom*, Israel's word for peace. Again we can refer to Klassen's *Love of Enemies* wherein he refers to Von Rad's insistence that *shalom* refers to a social reality.[18] Commenting on the Matthean beatitude designating peacemakers as sons or children of God, Klassen gives helpful background from the Hebrew scriptures illustrating how Matthew sees the Messiah, savior of the world, as a peacemaker.[19]

Each time the risen Jesus greeted his disciples with "Peace," some reference to his sufferings is also mentioned. In the Matthean Gospel, the "half-overjoyed, half-fearful" women were told by the angel, "I know you are looking for Jesus, the crucified, but he is not here" (Mt. 28:5f). The Lucan account emphasizes twice, both at Emmaus and at Jerusalem, that the Messiah must suffer (Lk. 24:26,46). John's Gospel highlights the wounds of Jesus (Jn. 20:19f, 26f). All these reminders of the sufferings and death of Jesus speak of the great saving activity of God whereby death and all that leads to it were definitively overcome. The risen Jesus was able to give the gift of God's own peace as he had promised in the supper discourse (Jn. 14:27f). The risen Jesus could enable his disciples to become peacemakers. But first those disciples, beginning to grasp the intrinsic relation between suffering in love and wondrous new life, had to accept Jesus' gift of peace and his challenge of peacemaking.

Characteristically, Jesus gave his disciples a bit of time before he visited them again on the lakeshore and called them children. Is it too much to suppose this new title implied those disciples had accepted Jesus' gift of peace and his challenge to become peacemakers? On this occasion Jesus didn't have to offer peace one more time. Instead, he called his disciples children, the name Matthew associates with the peacemaker Beatitude (Mt. 5:9). Once again, let us recall the setting. Jesus called his peacemakers children in the context of an occasion which insured a new spirit of joy, of play, and of forgiving love would be associated with the making of peace.

That picnic meal ended with one of the most endearing and important scenes in all of the stories of the risen Jesus (Jn. 21:15f). Alone with Peter, Jesus completed his teachings on authority which held so much prominence during his passion.

On the basis of love, nothing more, nothing less, Peter was entrusted with authoritative power. Again, the note of suffering was sounded when Peter's death was hinted at and the invitation was given by Jesus, "Follow me" (Jn. 21:19). When one recalls the continual peace motif running through all the resurrection texts, could that invitation to follow Jesus ever be taken seriously apart from its peacemaking implications?

Every Gospel episode relating an appearance of the risen Jesus carries the element of surprise. Mary Magdalen and the other women, the two Emmaus travelers, and the other groups of disciples who encountered the risen Jesus were all taken by surprise. Perhaps the most surprising story of all is the account of Saul converted to Paul on the way to Damascus (Ac. 9:1f). More surprising than the event itself is the answer the blinded Saul received when he asked, "Who are you, Lord?" (Ac. 9:5). The risen Jesus responded by identifying himself with those suffering persecution.

The surprising identification of Jesus with suffering and persecuted Christians in the Damascus story is similar to the surprising identifications of Jesus with suffering persons in the Matthean account of the final judgment (Mt. 25:31f). In both accounts there is a mysterious oneness of suffering persons with the Lord Jesus. In the judgment scene, the sufferers are the hungry, the naked, the sick, and the imprisoned. In both situations, the saving of human life is the subject of Jesus' concern. In each of these stories, not only is there interwoven a bit of playful guessing which has its own way of alleviating tension and making room for peace, there is also a peacemaking technique, demonstrated by Jesus in the Pauline conversion account. Saul was definitely an "enemy" of Jesus. Before knowing the outcome of the Damascus encounter, one might readily conjecture that Saul would be struck dead, rather than blind. After all, this Saul was responsible for the imprisonment and death of many followers of Jesus.. Killing him would certainly be a way of preventing the killing of many other innocent persons. But in the Damascus episode, the risen Jesus witnessed to a most surprising way to encounter an "enemy."

In commenting on ways and means the followers of Jesus could use to "love enemies," Klassen points to the importance of taking "the initiative with a tactic of surprise going beyond what the enemy has done."[20] Klassen also insists that the peacemaker's actions of surprising initiative are planned and motivated by a compassionate love, one which always respects the enemy's freedom to respond positively or negatively. Paul went through an extraordinary conversion experience, one in which he freely accepted the invitation to follow Jesus as friend, no longer as enemy.

Reflecting on these resurrection stories from the viewpoint of playfulness as a way to peacemaking may seem a bit strange, perhaps even a bit farfetched. In such reflection it is necessary to appreciate that the playfulness of the risen Jesus is characterized by a surprising freedom along with childlike spontaneity and joy. Unfortunately, we are not accustomed to think of Jesus in this way. Consequently, we have deprived him of one of the most attractive aspects of his human personality, a way in which he images most profoundly the playfulness of the creating Logos. Furthermore, by neglecting playfulness in the human life of Jesus, particularly in his risen life, we are ignoring one of the most necessary aspects of effective peacemaking.

During the first three centuries of the Christian era, one of the persons who grasped the significance of the playfulness and the peacemaking witness of Jesus was Clement of Alexandria. Delightful Christian humanist, Clement knew that much of the wisdom of his Greek culture, including its playful music and drama, found new and fulfilling expression in Jesus. In *Gods and Games* Miller contends that Clement heads the list of all theologians whose lifestyle and writings prefigured a contemporary theology of play.[21] Hugo Rahner also highlights Clement's appreciation of the role of playfulness in Christian life. In his chapter, "The Playing of Man," Rahner quotes Clement directly by way of illustration:

Joyful is the spirit of those
who are children in Christ
and order their lives with patient perseverance.
This indeed is the playing of the children of God![22]

Thomas Merton translated selections from Clement's *The Protreptikos* in which Clement hails Jesus not only as the Word, but as the New Song. After elaborating on the musical power of several Greek mythical heroes, Clement writes, "Very different from the mythical singer is the one I now propose to you . . .

See what power the new song has!
From stones, men,
From beasts it has made men.
Those otherwise dead,
Those without a share in life
      that is really life
At the mere sound of this song
Have come back to life . . .
Moreover He has structured the whole universe musically
And the discord of elements He has brought together
      in an ordered symphony
So that the whole Cosmos is for Him in harmony."[23]

As this treatise continues, Clement refers to the custom of making music to initiate a battle. Then using scriptural military imagery, Clement deftly contrasts Christ's summon for peacemaking.

Now the trumpet sounds with a mighty voice calling
the soldiers of the world to arms, announcing war:
And shall not Christ who has uttered His summons
      to peace even to the ends of the earth
Summon together His own soldiers of peace?
Indeed, O Man, He has called to arms with His Blood
and His Word an army that sheds no blood:

> To these soldiers He had handed over the Kingdom
>   of Heaven.
> The trumpet of Christ is His Gospel. He has sounded
>   it in our ears.
> And we have heard Him.
> Let us be armed for peace, putting on the armor of
>   justice, seizing the shield of faith,
> The helmet of salvation,
> And sharpening the "sword of the spirit which is the
>   Word of God."[24]

Clement's incipient peacemaking Christology has much to offer us today. His cosmic vision can speak directly to our concern for global survival. His playful spirit and aesthetic appreciation can inspire our imaginative efforts for creating new images and symbols, so necessary for all peacemaking efforts.

To move from Clement of Alexandria to our own day is to move from the period of history in which the Christian stance against participation in warfare was strong and clear, to a period in which that basic Gospel stance of peacemaking is becoming more and more urgent. *The Challenge of Peace* is very explicit in its insistence on the risen Jesus, the Lord of history, as source of hope and strength for today's Christians who must face the pressing challenge of peacemaking in a nuclear age (#2). With Clement and all Christians down through the ages who have held fast to the truth that the risen Jesus "has called to arms with His Blood and His word an army that sheds no blood," a lifestyle encompassing "the playing of the children of God" has had significant influence on the peacemaking efforts of those followers of Jesus. A few final comments on this "playing of the children of God," to quote Clement once again, will serve as concluding remarks to this consideration of playfulness and peacemaking.

Play is intrinsic to cultural development. So wrote Johan Huizinga in his classic work *Homo Ludens*, subtitled *A Study of the Play Element in Culture*. Without any qualifications, Huizinga stated "in the absence of the play-spirit civilization is impossible."[25] In his concluding chapter he insisted, "We have gradually become convinced that civilization is rooted in noble play and that, if it is to unfold in full dignity and style, it cannot afford to neglect the play-element. The observance of play-rules is nowhere more imperative than in the relations between countries and States. Once they are broken, society falls into barbarism and chaos."[26] No one needs to take such insightful words to heart more than Christian peacemakers. Moving from a warmaking world into one of peacemaking calls for a cultural transformation of the highest order. "Will we make it?" asked Harvey Cox. "Will we move into this world of revitalized celebration and creative imagination? Or will we destroy ourselves with nuclear bombs or man-made plagues?"[27]

A playful spirit of celebration is finding expression in more and more peacemaking efforts. One historic example is *The Ribbon*, a national and international sewing project which originated in the prayerful mind and heart of one woman, Justine Merrit, who invited others to help her "tie up" the Pentagon. This ribbon, created by thousands of persons, mostly women, was made of artistically sewn segments depicting "What I cannot bear to think of as lost forever in a nuclear war." In August 1985, forty years after the bombings of Hiroshima and Nagasaki, fifteen miles of ribbon, portraying beautiful and precious persons and things of God's creation, encircled not only the Pentagon, but the Capitol and the White House Ellipse as well. Thousands of persons joined in celebrating their hopes for a future without war, a future with a world which has created workable ways for making peace. Several States also had Ribbon celebrations at their state capitols. On hearing of this project, some persons laughed in scorn; many more smiled in joy. Justine described the event as a great party for peace.[28]

Many other examples of people creating playful, celebrating ways to initiate peacemaking could be cited, from the paper cranes project of Hiroshima children to a baseball game of conscientious objector students with their classmates in the ROTC. In such situations the spirit of play with its joy and surprise has begun to dispel tension and hostility and has made the way for a friendly spirit of dialog. Granted, these efforts of ordinary people may seem totally insignificant in the face of superpower "defense" plans and nuclear war strategies. But the words of Dwight Eisenhower are apropos here. "People want peace so much that one of these days governments had better get out of the way and let them have it."[29]

More recently, the noted moral theologian Richard McCormick has commented on the moral rights which people have to be part of the decision-making process pertaining to nuclear war. After all, it is the ordinary people who are the prospective victims of nuclear holocaust. Furthermore, McCormick pointed to the growing number of ordinary people in mass movements throughout Europe and the United States with respect to peacemaking.[30] In those people empowered by the Spirit of the risen Jesus, whether they realize it or not, lies genuine hope for a future in which the ways of peace will overcome the ways of war.

The risen Jesus is our pledge of a new and different future, one characterized by Jesus' gift of peace. In the Gospel stories, including those of Jesus' risen life, we can find needed clues to the ways and means of bringing that future into existence. Surprising as it may seem at first, the joy of the risen Jesus breaks forth in a spirit of play. Entering into that same spirit of play helps persons and communities and nations make room for the gift of God's own peace. Without a doubt, playfulness is one of the great gifts the risen Son of God, the creating Logos, wants to share with his disciples as together they participate in the creative process of making a peaceful world.

Footnotes

[1] One of the most helpful recent studies treating briefly the major questions surrounding the New Testament resurrection stories is Raymond Brown's *The Virginal Conception & Bodily Resurrection of Jesus* (New York: Paulist Press 1973).

[2] Johan Huizinga's *Homo Ludens, A Study of the Play Element in Culture* (Boston: The Beacon Press 1955) is a major work on the role of play in cultural development. More recent studies focusing more specifically on a theology of play include the following: Hugo Rahner, *Man at Play*, tr. Brian Battershaw and Edward Quinn (New York: Herder and Herder 1967); Harvey Cox, *The Feast of Fools* (Cambridge, Mass.: Harvard University Press 1969); Robert E. Neale, *In Praise of Play, Toward a Psychology of Religion* (New York: Harper & Row 1969); David L. Miller, *Gods and Games, Toward a Theology of Play* (New York: the World Publishing Company 1970). Miller includes a discussion of the importance of play theology for theology itself. He suggests, "The application of the game/play terms to religious matters may indeed be a word game. But in such an academic theological game there might be discovered, not only the religious dimension in man's play, not only the playful dimension in man's religions, but 'a way of preserving or restoring' the life of theologies which have been seen as irrelevant to modern experience and of the gods whose deaths have been recently announced." p. 91.

[3] Neale, *In Praise*, p. 24.

[4] Neale, *In Praise*, p. 22. Neale's approach to play illustrates the problem of distorted play in much of contemporary culture. Fierce competition, commercialization of sports, passive spectator roles, and increasing violence in games, including video games, contribute to undermining genuine play and its possibilities for "re-creation" of persons and communities.

[5] Neale, *In Praise*, p. 122f.

[6] Neale, *In Praise*, p. 174.

[7] Rahner, *Man*, p. 65f.

[8] Rahner, *Man*, p. 7f.

[9] Rahner, *Man*, p. xiv.

[10] Rahner, *Man*, Ch.1, "The Playing of God."

[11] Rahner, *Man*, p. 24f.

[12] Neale, *In Praise*, p. 166.

[13] Miller, *Gods*, p. 131.

[14] Rahner, *Man*, p. 23, quoting Gregory Nazianzen, *Carmina*, I,2,2, vv. 598-90 (PG 37, 624Af). Although this translation is not the most accurate of the key text of Proverbs 8:31 emphasizing the playing of Wisdom in the creative process, nevertheless this translation captures the element of God's playfulness in creating the world.

[15] *Ibid.*, quoting Cornelius a Lapide, *Commentaria in Proverbia* 8.31, (Nota tertio, Mystice).

[16] Jon Sobrino, *Christology at the Crossroads*, tr. John Drury (Maryknoll: Orbis 1978) p. 105.

[17] One of the most helpful studies in this regard is Walter Brueggemann's *Living Toward a Vision: Biblical Reflections on Shalom* (Philadelphia: United Church Press 1976, 1982).

[18] William Klassen, *Love of Enemies* (Philadelphia: Fortress Press 1984) p. 40.

[19] Klassen, *Love*, p. 74f.

[20] Klassen, *Love*, p. 86.

[21] Miller, *Gods*, p. 164.

[22] Rahner, *Man*, p. 44, quoting Clement of Alexandria, *Paedagogus*, I, 5, 21, 3-4 (GCS I, pp. 102-3).

[23] Thomas Merton, *Clement of Alexandria, Selections from The Protreptikos, An Essay and Translation*, (Norfolk, CT: A New Directions Book 1962) p. 17f.

[24] Merton, *Clement*, p. 27.

[25] Huizinga, *Homo*, p. 101.

[26] Huizinga, *Homo*, p. 210.

[27] Cox, *The Feast*, p. 162.

[28] As The Ribbon project developed into a nationwide endeavor, a national newsletter served as a major means of communication along with several bulletins in various states throughout the country. Several states had coordinators for the project. A book depicting some of the most beautiful ribbon banners was entitled, *The Ribbon: A Celebration of Life*, published by Lark Books, Asheville, NC. Ribbons are permanently displayed in various museums throughout the United States, including Chicago's Peace Museum.

[29] As quoted in *The Ribbon-Illinois*, May, 1985 bulletin.

[30] Richard A. McCormick, "Nuclear Deterrence and the Problem of Intention: A Review of the Positions," in Philip J. Murnion, ed., *Catholics and Nuclear War* (New York: Crossroad 1983) pp. 169, 179.

5. Programming for Peace

Programming for peace may sound like computer language, especially to persons very aware of the computer programming for war which is one of the most frightening aspects of nuclear technology. Obviously, the Jesus of the Gospels was not engaged in developing computer programs. But the Jesus of the Gospels is pictured as a person with a vision for a new world order, even a whole new creation. Furthermore, the Jesus of the Gospels has a sense of practical implementation. Jesus in his teaching mission is presented as a leader who inspires and challenges the people into startlingly new ways of living, new ways of action. The Jesus of the Gospels does initiate a program of action for peacemaking.

Jesus' program for peacemaking is expounded primarily in the grouping of lessons found in the Matthean Sermon on the Mount with its parallel section in the Lucan Sermon on the Plain. Early on in *The Challenge of Peace* reference is made to this significant teaching of Jesus. "The Catholic tradition on war and peace is a long and complex one, reaching from the Sermon on the Mount to the statements of Pope John Paul II" (#7).

Before examining aspects of this "long and complex tradition" so often centering on the Sermon on the Mount, a reminder is in order regarding the methodology of this particular study. As indicated in Chapter One, the early Christians understood the teachings of Jesus in the light of the entire passion experience,

including the resurrection. From that perspective they proclaimed and composed the good news, the Gospel. From this
same perspective of the passion narrative, let us turn our attention now to those particular peacemaking techniques and programs of Jesus found in the Sermon on the Mount.

Contemporary scripture scholarship has enabled us to understand both the Matthean Sermon on the Mount and the Lucan
Sermon on the Plain as summations of many teachings of
Jesus.[1] Joachim Jeremias' brief study, *The Sermon on the
Mount*, is invaluable in this regard.[2] Jeremias emphasizes how
Jesus' teaching as presented in both Matthew and Luke "burst
the bounds of late Judaism"[3] and presented "symptoms, signs,
and examples" of the kingdom breaking into the world.[4] All the
sayings of Jesus presented in these Gospel passages depend on
his lived example for their validity.

Contrary to several scholarly opinions, Jeremias rejects the
theories of 'impossible ideal' and 'interim ethic' pertaining solely
to the final end time. Rather, he makes a convincing case for
a pre- and post-baptismal catechesis explaining the implications of Christian faith lived authentically. Jeremias concludes
that the Beatitudes in both Gospels are an introductory statement, a *protasis* keynoting the themes of the entire Sermon.

Even a cursory comparison of the Matthean and Lucan
Beatitudes immediately points up the differences in numbers
and wording. Matthew gives us the more familiar list of eight
(or ten) while Luke gives four blessings and four contrasting
woes. Luke's omission of the peacemaker Beatitude at first
sight seems to pose a problem for a peacemaking Christology
and suggests some careful scrutiny is in order. But first, the
position of the peacemaker Beatitude in the Matthean listing
calls for special consideration in this study of Jesus,
peacemaker.

The peacemaker Beatitude comes close to the end of
Matthew's blessings. I doubt that such a scheme was incidental
or haphazard. A careful probing into the meaning of each
Beatitude indicates a progression in which the attitudes implied

in each successive blessing depend in no small way on the interiorization of the attitudes and outlooks expressed in the previous blessings. In Matthew's scheme, a plan for gradual maturing in Christian living is programmed into this teaching of Jesus. Peacemaking depends on a genuine poverty of spirit; on a compassionate, merciful, purified heart able to share suffering; on a gentle nonviolent approach to conflict; on a passionate hunger and thirst for justice. Of all the Beatitudes, peacemaking is the action beatitude which most closely identifies one as a member of God's own family, as one sharing the life and love of God.

Luke's omission of the peacemaker Beatitude per se, does not mean that Luke omits the issue of peacemaking. Immediately after the four woes, Luke gives a powerful treatise on love of enemies. As a matter of fact, the whole of Luke's Sermon (Lk. 6:17-49), much shorter than Matthew's (Mt. 5:1-7:29), focuses most heavily on love of enemies. It is in this context of love of enemies, so essential for peacemaking in all human relations, that Luke identifies who can be called children of God.

In comparison with Matthew, Luke substitutes those who love enemies for peacemakers, thereby practically identifying the two. Whereas Matthew writes, "Blest too the peacemakers; they shall be called sons (children) of God" (Mt. 5:9), Luke states, "Love your enemy and do good; lend without expecting repayment. Then will your recompense be great. You will rightly be called sons (children) of the Most High, since he himself is good to the ungrateful and the wicked" (Lk. 6:35).

Luke continues, associating compassionate love and forgiveness with a compasionate God. "Be compassionate, as your Father is compassionate. Do not judge, and you will not be judged. Do not condemn, and you will not be condemned. Pardon, and you shall be pardoned" (Lk. 6:36).

Particularly in Lucan theology, these teachings on compassionate love of enemies and forgiveness rely on the passion narrative for their validity. The Jesus who could cry out on the cross, "Father, forgive them" (Lk. 23:34), gave the necessary credibility to his difficult and demanding teachings on forgiveness and love of enemies as recorded in Luke's Sermon on the Plain.

Matthew's injunctions on lack of retaliation and love of enemies are similar to Luke's. Matthew identifies those who love enemies and pray for persecutors as "sons (children) of your heavenly Father, for his sun rises on the bad and the good, he rains on the just and the unjust" (Mt. 5:45).

In commenting on these passages from both Matthew and Luke, Klassen in *Love of Enemies*, mentions that Luke's illustrations show greater concern for the economic sphere.[5] Klassen also points out that all of the illustrations in both Gospels depend on the simple, strong, surprising command, "Love your enemies" (Mt. 5:44; Lk. 6:27, 35). This command admits of no ambiguity, even though the followers of Jesus through the centuries have managed to rationalize it away or to put severe limits on its practice.[6]

This central teaching of Jesus on love of enemies as key to peacemaking is treated with new perspective in one of the most significant early commentaries on the Sermon on the Mount, that of Augustine of Hippo. Considering Augustine's influence in establishing just war criteria for Christians, his teachings on this command of Jesus deserve critical examination.

To this day Augustine of Hippo exerts a major influence on the Christian conscience with respect to war and peace. In *The Challenge of Peace*, articles 81 and 82, in the section entitled "The Just War Criteria," refer to Augustine explicitly. Article 81 summarizes his thinking in the following way.

> Historically and theologically the clearest answer to the question is found in St. Augustine. Augustine was impressed by the fact and the consequences of sin in history — the "not yet" dimension of the kingdom. In his view war was both the result of sin and a tragic remedy for sin in the life of political societies.

War arose from disordered ambitions, but it could also be used, in some cases at least, to restrain evil and protect the innocent. The classic case which illustrated his view was the use of lethal force to prevent aggression against innocent victims. Faced with the fact of attack on the innocent, the presumption that we do no harm, even to our enemy, yielded to the command of love understood as the need to restrain an enemy who would injure the innocent.[7]

Contemporary scholars reinforce the bishops' assertion about Augustine's influence on the morality of war. In his recent book, *The Early Fathers on War and Military Service*, patristic scholar Louis J. Swift claims,

No writer of the early Church contributed more to the development of Christian attitudes regarding war, violence and military service than St. Augustine. As the one who is commonly credited with being the author of the "theory of the just war" and the only theologian in the early centuries of Christianity to endorse and to discuss openly the use of coercion for suppressing religious dissent, he occupies a critical position in the history of the problem.[8]

Swift also makes it very clear that Augustine really does not give us a carefully refined theory of a just war, and certainly not a 'doctrine' of a just war. Rather the attitudes and approach of Augustine toward a just war are more accurate descriptions of the heritage he has left us.

Especially in the light of today's emphasis on experiential data as a base for theological thought, it is important to recall Augustine's own experience of war. He lived through the period of Alaric's sack of Rome in 410 A.D. During the final years of Augustine's life, the invasion of the Vandal armies into North Africa threatened his own city of Hippo.

Augustine's widespread influence on this question of war and peace must also be considered in the light of his extraordinary authority in his own lifetime and in subsequent centuries of Christian life. Few persons can claim all his credentials as philosopher, theologian, authority in the spiritual life, bishop, prolific writer, and canonized saint. Indeed, Augustine is a giant to be reckoned with. His teachings on war have held major sway in the Christian community for over 1500 years.

In Augustine's day and for centuries afterwards, sermons and catechetical instructions were the major media on which the ordinary people, mostly illiterate, depended for a clearer understanding of their life of faith. Augustine has been called "the universal model for preachers in the Middle Ages."[9] Furthermore, Jaroslav Pelikan claims that Augustine's explanation of the Sermon on the Mount dominated medieval exegesis until Thomas Aquinas and beyond; Luther still used Augustine's work when he wrote his own *Commentary on the Sermon on the Mount* in 1530-32.[10]

Augustine's *Exposition of the Sermon on the Mount* was written in 393, soon after his ordination to the priesthood. The *Exposition* is a verse by verse commentary comprising one book on Matthew's fifth chapter and a second book for chapters six and seven.

In his treatment of the peacemaker Beatitude, Augustine emphasizes interior peace resulting from the contemplation of truth. Paralleling the Beatitudes with the seven gifts of the Holy Spirit, Augustine associates this peacemaker Beatitude with wisdom, a gift which enables one to be like God, to become a child of God.[11] All things are in proper order with peacemakers; "no passion is in rebellion against reason, but everything is in submission to man's spirit because that spirit is obedient to God."[12]

Considering Augustine's later teachings on justifying war, it is significant that this commentary on the peacemaking Beatitude makes no explicit mention of peacemaking in the societal order. However, even in our own century Augustine's approach to the challenge of peacemaking sounded in this

Beatitude has been re-echoed. Gerald Vann's *Divine Pity*, sub-titled *A Study in the Social Implications of the Beatitudes*, relates each Beatitude to a specific Sacrament and culminates the entire work with a chapter on "The Love of Peace" in which the Sacrament of Priesthood is highlighted. Written in the for-ties while the Second World War was still raging, this treatment of peace concentrates on wisdom and contemplation in similar fashion to Augustine. No allusion is made to the Beatitude's societal peacemaking challenge in a wartorn world even though the book claims to be concerned with social implications.[13]

In the light of today's new awakening to the challenge of peacemaking in all aspects of life including international rela-tions, Augustine's comments on love of enemies are most per-tinent. In a one-to-one relationship, Augustine counsels recog-nizing an enemy as a fellow human being. Such a recognition means wishing the same good fortune for this person as one would wish for oneself. Augustine then explains, "This means that he wishes him to be corrected of his faults, to become a new man, and thus to enter the kingdom of heaven."[14]

As the *Exposition* continues, this concern for correcting faults moves into a justification of punishment. In Augustine's own words,

> A punishment that is designed for the purpose of correction is not hereby forbidden; for that very punishment is an exercise of mercy, and is not incom-patible with the firm resolve by which we are ready to suffer even further injuries from a man whose amendment we desire. But no one is fit for the task of inflicting such punishment unless — by the great-ness of his love — he has overcome the hate by which those who seek to avenge themselves are usually enraged.[15]

Two important factors emerge in this text. Not only is "punishment for the purpose of correction" justified, but also the fact of proper motivation and right intention begin to play an important role in Augustine's teaching. He elaborates

further, stating that the punishment may be inflicted only by
a person in rightly constituted authority and it must be inflicted
"as affectionately as a father would punish his little child."[16]
In summation, Augustine states that the intention must be "to
make the offender happy by a correction, rather than unhappy
by a punishment" and the punishing person must be willing to
suffer further injuries calmly.[17]

Throughout this *Exposition* Augustine appeals to many passages from the Hebrew Scriptures, including references to the
prophets. Elijah is singled out as a "noble and saintly" man
who, with authority from God, inflicted death as a punishment
for sin. Furthermore, in such situations Augustine claims,
"Those who were put to death did not suffer the injury from
death itself; rather they were suffering injury from sin, and it
might have become worse if they had continued to live."[18]

In fairness to Augustine, it must be said that he lacked the
tools and the fruits of contemporary scripture scholarship so
readily at our disposal. Today, in sharp contrast to Augustine,
Klassen comments on Elijah in a section of *Love of Enemies*
entitled "Jesus and Samaritan Vengeance." Particularly after
the Transfiguration account in which Jesus discourses with
Elijah and Moses, does Jesus move to a whole new way of living,
a way of love which leads to the cross.[19] Klassen then adds
that far too often in its history the church has treated enemies
more in the spirit of Elijah than in the spirit of Jesus.[20] How
great a role Augustine played in promoting such a vengeful
Elijah spirit is hard to determine precisely. But when Augustine
faces the question of 'enemies' in the societal order, much of
his early thinking on punishment as presented in the *Exposition
on the Sermon on the Mount* is repeated and expanded.

Augustine's views on a God who punishes through war are
rooted in his theological background. For Augustine, a warrior
God is a punishing God. This image of God punishing sometimes
even by means of war is a prominent one for Augustine in many
of his writings, and seems to correlate with his profound conviction of the all-pervasive character of original sin.

In the very first section of *The City of God*, written approximately twenty years after the *Exposition on the Sermon on the Mount*, Augustine claims God "regularly uses wars as a way of chastising and punishing sinful individuals and of testing through afflictions like this, men who lead a just and praiseworthy life" (DCD 1.1).[21] Later on, Augustine attributes the duration of wars to God, also in the context of punishment and testing. In Chapter Five of *The City of God* he writes, "Thus also the duration of wars are determined by Him as He may see meet, according to His righteous will, and pleasure, and mercy, to afflict or to console the human race, so that they are sometimes of longer, sometimes of shorter duration" (DCD 5.22).

In addition to war Augustine includes several other institutional means of punishment which he enumerates in one of his letters to Macedonius, Vicar of Africa.

> Surely it is not in vain that we have such institutions as the power of the king, the death penalty of the judge, the hooks of the executioner, the weapons of the soldier, the stringency of the overlord and even the strictness of a good father. When they are feared, evil men are held in check, and the good enjoy greater peace among the wicked. (L.153.6.16)[22]

This conviction of the need for various means of punishment including the death penalty and war seems to have deepened in Augustine as a result of the Donatist controversies. Some of the North African bishops apparently revived their communities through various threats and means of coercion. Reflecting on that situation Augustine remarked,

> The difficulty or pain a man endures serves as an incentive to him to think about the reasons for his suffering. The purpose of it all is that if he discovers that he is suffering for justice's sake, he might embrace the good involved in undergoing such torments on behalf of justice. On the other hand, if he discovers

that what motivates his suffering is actually evil and
that his difficulties and trials are wasted, he might
change his attitude for the better and, in one stroke,
free himself both from useless torments and from
the iniquity itself that will do him much more griev-
ous harm.[23]

Before leaving these brief samplings of Augustinian texts
commenting on God's use of war or other means of coercion as
punishment or as testing, it should be noted again that the
motivational factor in such punitive actions is of utmost importance. In pondering Augustine's teaching on war and punishment, sometimes it's difficult to remember he is a theologian
known for his emphasis on God as love. That central point in
his theology is not forgotten in his 'guidelines' for war. Agreeing
with his teacher Ambrose, Augustine claimed that violence
and an internal spirit of love are neither incompatible nor mutu-
ally exclusive.[24]

One final letter of Augustine deserves mention because of
the way it treats of an interior disposition in the context of
peace and peacemaking by referring directly to the Sermon on
the Mount. Significantly, this letter was written to another
government official, this time to Count Boniface, governor of
Africa.

Peace should be your aim; war should be a matter
of necessity so that God might free you from necessity
and preserve you in peace. One does not pursue peace
in order to wage war; he wages war to achieve peace.
And so, even in the act of waging war be careful to
maintain a peaceful disposition so that by defeating
your foes you can bring them the benefits of peace.
'Blessed are the peacemakers,' says the Lord, 'for
they will be called the children of God' (Mt. 5:9).

If peace is such a delightful dimension of man's tem-
poral happiness, how much sweeter is the divine

peace that belongs to the eternal happiness of angels.
And so, let it be of necessity rather than your own
desire that you kill the enemy fighting against you.
(L.189.6)[25]

It is hardly an exaggeration to say that Augustine's rationale
for punishing enemies has been far more prevalent in Christian
thought and action than the straightforward Gospel example
and teaching of Jesus to lovingly forgive enemies as a necessary
grounding of all peacemaking efforts. How many devious ways
and means have been invented by Christians to punish those
perceived as enemies for whatever reasons? How many times
do we still hear Christian people profess their belief in waging
war to achieve peace? As for a right intention in this punishing,
often warmaking process, I remember only too well the many
discussions we had during World War II. As young people faced
with the immediate prospect of going to war, we asked in utmost
sincerity, how we could love someone and then proceed to kill
them. I doubt if we ever quoted Augustine to support our
rationalizations. But I know we did not face squarely the implications of Jesus' command to love our enemies.

Augustine lived at a pivotal point in history as far as Christian attitudes toward war and peace are concerned. In the
fourth century the majority of Christians made a tragic shift
away from Jesus' peacemaking Beatitude with its implications
for reconciliation with enemies. Christian involvement in war
has accelerated ever since. But today we can rejoice that our
own period of history is beginning to witness another major
shift in Christian consciousness of the Gospel imperative for
peacemaking as found in the Sermon on the Mount. We are in
the early stages of a radical renewal of Gospel ways and means
for the making of peace.

In the sixties, a series of sermons on the Beatitudes was
preached in the Cathedral of Cologne, a city bearing brutal
scars of the Second World War. In commenting on the
peacemaker Beatitude, the preacher did raise the question of
the church's responsibility for political peace.[26]

More recently, Michael Crosby's *Spirituality of the Beatitudes* directly confronted the questions of modern warfare and peacemaking possibilities in his treatment of the peacemaker Beatitude. In describing prevailing ideologies which provoke war, Crosby asserted, "The first step in any conflict is to perceive the opponent in terms of the *diabolical enemy-image*. The other is seen as diametrically opposed to what one represents . . . To stop such a diabolical enemy, strong steps (must) be taken."[27] Such an ideology is challenged by Crosby in the light of Jesus' Gospel command to "love your enemies."

Perhaps no contemporary writer has written more convincingly on the need to restore an authentic Beatitude spirituality to the Christian community than Eileen Egan in her superb essay, "Beatitudes, Works of Mercy, and Pacifism." After describing war's total reversal of the works of mercy enjoined by the Beatitudes, a reversal which not only starves the hungry rather than feeding them but also systematically despoils their croplands, Egan points to the complete impossibility of performing any of the works of mercy in a situation of nuclear war. Referring directly to the just war tradition, Egan insightfully decries its incompatibility with the Sermon on the Mount when she wrote, " . . . the most tragic aspect of the operation of 'just war' thinking is that it effectively displaced love from its centrality in the Christian message and robbed Christianity of its most distinctive teaching, love of enemy."[28]

In writing *The Challenge of Peace*, the Catholic bishops of the United States emphasized that "the unique dangers and dynamics of the nuclear arms race present qualitatively new problems which must be addressed by fresh applications of traditional moral principles" (#13). The bishops also declared that "limiting the resort to force in human affairs . . . is not a sufficient response to Vatican II's challenge 'to undertake a completely fresh reappraisal of war'" (#23).

These calls for a "completely fresh reappraisal of war" and "fresh applications of traditional moral principles" beckon us once again to the Sermon on the Mount wherein we can find the heart of Jesus' teaching on peacemaking. Peacemaking necessitates forgiveness and love of enemies. When New Testament scholar Donald Senior wrote on enemy love as "Jesus' Most Scandalous Teaching," he referred to Matthew and Luke's texts not as peripheral teaching, but as the heart of Jesus' message.[29]

Jesus' programming for peace, centering on love of enemies, is exceedingly practical and eminently possible because of the empowering of the very same Spirit whose love animated Jesus' own forgiveness. Today more than ever as we face the real possibility of nuclear holocaust, the urgent challenge of peacemaking demands a renewal of Beatitude spirituality. This renewal will necessitate a drastic reform of centuries-old justifications for wars in which enemies were punished even unto death. In unprecedented ways, we are challenged to become peacemakers, those children of God who love as the only-begotten Son of God asks us to, even as he loves us (Jn. 15:12).

In our times, to put such major focus on love of enemies as basic to all peacemaking may seem totally unrealistic in the face of governmental projections for more and more weapons of unimaginable destruction, to say nothing of repeated stalemates at peace talks. Furthermore, through the media the average person is exposed constantly to fearsome statements about the nation's enemies. The threats of communist takeovers seem to abound everywhere. As ordinary people share their hopes and fears for a peaceful future, time and again the question is raised, "But what about the Russians?" In this context of the real world, does Jesus' peacemaking emphasis on love of enemies make any sense?

Jesus' programming for peacemaking as given in the Sermon on the Mount makes sense only in light of his passion experience. As the political and military enemies of his own Jewish people were putting him to a most cruel death, Jesus prayed for forgiveness, an action which demanded unbelievable love of enemies. Vengeful retaliations and punishments were not even considered. Jesus on the cross was peacemaker par excellence, a realization proclaimed by the early church in the Epistle to the Ephesians (Eph. 2:13f).

Witnessing to the truth and power of loving forgiveness of enemies struck right at the roots of enmity. Jesus knew that. He knew that any other attempts at reconciliation which did not stem from this radical forgiving love of enemies could not sustain a lasting peaceful relation. His program for peacemaking was not a superficial one. Detailed negotiations would have to be worked out. But all those details would be effective only if the underlying attitude was one of loving forgiveness.

The scarred history of the human family testifies to the wisdom of Jesus. Tragically, this testimony is predominantly negative, as vengeance and retaliation have held sway. One of the worst examples of the escalation of enemy hate was the retaliation bombings of Germany in World War II when the new military objective had little to do with the movement of troops, but had everything to do with breaking the enemy's (the whole population's) will to resist.[30] Then came Hiroshima and Nagasaki.

Today, a rapidly growing number of Christians are joining the centuries-old testimony of the members of Peace Churches in their unqualified acceptance of Jesus' command to love enemies in the political order. May this new momentum for peacemaking increase with utmost speed and strength. All the other programmings for peace depend on it.

Footnotes

[1] For a scholarly presentation on the Hebraic background of the Sermon on the Mount see W.D. Davies, *The Setting of the Sermon on the Mount* (Cambridge: University Press 1964).

[2] Joachim Jeremias, *The Sermon on the Mount*, tr. Norman Perrin (Philadelphia: Fortress Press 1963).

[3] Jeremias, *The Sermon*, p. 6.

[4] Jeremias, *The Sermon*, p. 33.

[5] William Klassen, *Love of Enemies* (Philadelphia: Fortress Press 1984) p. 76.

[6] Klassen, *Love*, p. 84f. Klassen's entire chapter on "Jesus as Prince of Peace" includes a superb exegesis on the Sermon on the Mount.

[7] National Conference of Catholic Bishops, *The Challenge of Peace: God's Promise and Our Response* (Washington, DC: United States Catholic Conference, 1983) p. 26.

[8] Louis J. Swift, *The Early Fathers on War and Military Service* (Wilmington, DE: Michael Glazier, Inc. 1983) p. 110.

[9] Saint Augustine, *Commentary on the Lord's Sermon on the Mount with Seventeen Related Sermons*, tr. Denis J. Kavanagh (New York: Fathers of the Church, Inc. 1951) "Introduction," p. 15.

[10] Jaroslav Pelikan, ed., *The Preaching of Augustine*, "Our Lord's Sermon on the Mount" (Philadelphia: Fortress Press 1973) p. xvi.

[11] Augustine, *Commentary*, p. 26.

[12] Augustine, *Commentary*, p. 28.

[13] Gerald Vann, *The Divine Pity* (New York: Sheed and Ward 1946), Chapter Seven, "The Love of Peace," pp. 190-220.

[14] Augustine, *Commentary*, p. 62.

[15] Augustine, *Commentary*, p. 89.

[16] Augustine, *Commentary*, p. 90.

[17] *Ibid.*

[18] *Ibid.*

[19] *Klassen, Love*, p. 83.

[20] Klassen, *Love*, p. 84.

[21] Quoted in Swift, *The Early*, p. 121.

[22] Quoted in Swift, *The Early*, p. 112.

[23] Quoted in Swift, *The Early*, p. 143. (Reconsiderations 2.84).

[24] Swift, *The Early*, p. 123.

[25] Quoted in Swift, *The Early*, pp. 114f.

[26] Cf. Urban Warner Plotzke, *God's Own Magna Charta*, tr. J. Holland Smith (Westminster, Md: Newman Press 1963) p. 177f.

[27] Michael Crosby, *The Spirituality of the Beatitudes* (Maryknoll: Orbis 1981) p. 185.

[28] Eileen Egan, "Beatitudes, Works of Mercy, and Pacifism," in Thomas A. Shannon, ed., *War or Peace? The Search for New Answers* (Maryknoll: Orbis 1980) p. 184.

[29] Donald Senior, "Jesus' Most Scandalous Teaching," in John Pawlikowski and Donald Senior, eds., *Biblical and Theological Reflections on The Challenge of Peace* (Wilmington, De: Michael Glazier, Inc. 1984) p. 61. Also see Mary Evelyn Jegen, *How You Can Be a Peacemaker* (Liguori: Liguori Publications 1985), Chapter One, "The Teaching of Jesus on Love and Nonviolence."

[30] Roland Bainton, *The Christian Attitudes Toward War and Peace* (New York: Abingdon Press 1960) p. 225.

6. Preludes to Peacemaking

Preludes are very important. Literally speaking a prelude is an 'introduction to playing' and is usually associated with a musical composition. Preludes keynote the major themes of an entire musical score.

Preludes to peacemaking also pertain to playing — the playing characteristic of the children of God as described in Chapter Four of this study. Now by way of conclusion, three preludes to peacemaking will be considered: the Lucan infancy narrative; the early peacemaker Christological statement in the Epistle to the Ephesians; the early sacramental practice relating to peacemaking. In theological terms, these preludes are sounded in biblical, systematic, and sacramental theology, wherein a resounding pastoral harmonization for peacemaking is heard.

The Lucan infancy narrative which introduces the Gospel of Luke is a carefully constructed prelude to the peacemaking emphasis in all of Lucan theology. In pondering this emphasis on peacemaking, it is important to recall that the infancy narrative was the last part of Luke-Acts to be written.[1] From the vantage points of the entire third Gospel and Acts, this prelude was composed to give an orientation to a theology concerned with the church's mission to the Gentile world.[2] The theology of the Lucan infancy narrative is above all a Christology proclaiming both the humanity and the divinity of Jesus of Nazareth who is the center of salvation history.[3] Commenting on the structural pattern of the infancy narrative in his monumental work *The Birth of the Messiah*, Raymond Brown wrote, "The reader will discover that rarely has theology been dramatized with more artistry and delicacy."[4]

A musical motif characteristic of preludes is easily recognizable in the four songs inserted into Luke's infancy narrative. The three canticles, commonly referred to by their Latin titles, Magnificat (Lk. 1:46-55), Benedictus (Lk. 1:68-79) and Nunc Dimittis (Lk. 2:29-32), are complemented by the song of the angels at Jesus' birth (Lk. 2:14). The three canticles probably come from an early Jewish-Christian liturgical source;[5] the angels' song is probably a Lucan composition.[6]

The messianic focus of these Lucan songs highlights the themes of justice and peace. Relying heavily on the messianic theology so familiar to the early Jewish-Christian communities, the Lucan songs sound those messianic promises of the prophets and psalms which identify God's ways of salvation with new ways to peace. In the *Anchor Bible Commentary*, Joseph Fitzmyer goes so far as to claim that "peace became the mark of the awaited messianic kingdom."[7] From a Lucan perspective this peace seemed to combine elements of both *Pax Augusta* and Israel's *shalom*.[8] Klassen makes the important observation that Jesus' mission as bringer of peace is defined in political terms in the song Mary sings (Lk. 1:32,33). Jesus will be given the Davidic throne.[9]

Recent commentaries on Mary's Magnificat highlight the strong justice themes in this song. Writing from the vantage point of Argentina's poor, Arturo Paoli considers the Magnificat a resume of the entire Bible,[10] a song which "rises from the earth, out of a history bloodied by those who use power more for offense than defense of the right every one has to essential goods."[11]

From the peasant community of Solentiname, Nicaragua, come timely reflections on Mary's great song. One of the women, Esperanza, shared her understanding of the opening lines of Mary's prayer of praise. "She praises God because the Messiah is going to be born, and that's a great event for the people. She calls God 'Savior' because she knows that the Son that he has given her is going to bring liberation."[12] Another woman, Gloria, added, "She spoke for the future, it seems to me, because we are just barely beginning to see the liberation she announces."[13]

Not only in Latin America, but also in the United States we find renewed understanding of the power of Mary's Magnificat in a world crying out for justice and for peace. Two essays in *Mary According to Women* comment on the Magnificat. In "Mary, Mirror of Justice," Mary Donahey writes, "This desire to lessen the inequality between rich and poor appears to throb in Mary's heart, for she enters the New Testament scene proclaiming a Magnificat laden with justice implications."[14] The final essay, "Mary Immaculate, Woman of Freedom, Patroness of the United States" claims the Magnificat could be called a "canticle of freedom" because it "resonates with those persons in every generation whose hearts yearn for freedom from oppression of all kinds."[15]

As an early Jewish-Christian hymn, the Magnificat is a messianic song of justice because it sings of the new relationships the Messiah will establish. In Mary's Hebraic heritage, justice was above all a matter of fidelity to the relationship God intended.[16] True to the covenantal promise made to Abraham and to his faithful descendants, the Messiah, Mary's child, will reverse the unjust relationships which have caused untold suffering for the lowly and the hungry.

The Davidic messiah, proclaimed by the angel Gabriel (Lk. 1:26f), was described by Isaiah of Jerusalem as "Wonder-Counselor, God-Hero, Father-Forever, Prince of Peace" (Is. 9:5). His dominion would be "vast and forever peaceful" because "from David's throne and over his kingdom" he will confirm and sustain "judgment and justice, both now and forever" (Is. 9:6).[17]

The intrinsic relation between justice and peace is proclaimed with utmost clarity in one of Israel's great songs of praise. The psalmist sings:

I will hear what God proclaims:

the Lord — for he proclaims peace
To his people, and to his faithful ones,
     and to those who put in him their hope.
Near indeed is his salvation to those who
     fear him,
     glory dwelling in our land.
Kindness and truth shall meet;
     justice and peace shall kiss.
Truth shall spring out of the earth,
     and justice shall look down from heaven.
The Lord himself will give his benefits;
     our land shall yield its increase.
Justice shall walk before him,
     and salvation, along the way of his steps.
                              (Ps. 85:9-14)

These covenant themes of justice and peace resound in the
Lucan Canticles as the early Jewish-Christian community
praised God for sending Jesus, the Davidic Messiah who will
bring the covenant promises to fulfillment. If the Magnificat
can be considered a canticle of the justice and freedom characteristic of messianic times, then the Benedictus can be seen
primarily as a canticle of peace.

At first sight the Benedictus may seem to focus on John the
Baptist, rather than on Jesus. Considering Luke's use of parallelism in constructing the stories of the two annunciations, to
Zechariah and to Mary, Zechariah's Benedictus appropriately
would focus on John. However, a careful study of the text points
to Jesus as the person about whom the song is sung.[18]

The Benedictus climaxes with the proclamation of "the Dayspring" mercifully visiting his people, "to shine on those who
sit in darkness and in the shadow of death, to guide our feet
into the way of peace" (Lk. 1:78,79). This peace motif is repeated
when the angels sing at Jesus' birth, "Glory to God in high
heaven, peace on earth to those on whom God's favor rests"
(Lk. 2:14). Because Zechariah's song is modeled on the hymn

of praise in which the concluding verses often recapitulate the major themes of the entire hymn,[19] it is important to see how this canticle sings of the peacemaking ways of God. Throughout this hymn, God's covenant fidelity is praised. "He has visited and ransomed his people" (v. 68); he has raised a horn of saving strength" (v. 69); he has saved his people from their enemies (v. 71,74); he has dealt mercifully with them, remembering the holy covenant he made (v. 72). This newly born child, John, called prophet of the Most High, will go before the Lord to prepare straight paths (v. 76). In prophetic fashion, John will proclaim God's salvation in freedom from sin. Whatever else the way of peace may mean, it does mean that God takes the initiative in offering the strength of compassionate love in covenantal fidelity.

The image of a 'way' is very significant in Lucan theology, with its prominent journey motif both for Jesus and for his followers.[20] Two phrases in the Benedictus serve as preludes to this Lucan theology which appears in Acts as an early designation for Christians who were known as followers of the new way (Ac. 9:2; 19:9,23; 22:4; 24:14,22). Zechariah describes his newborn son's mission as preparing straight paths for the Lord (Lk. 1:76). The Lord Messiah would, in turn, guide his people "into the way of peace" (Lk. 1:79).

In addition to the "way" imagery, another significant image, the "Dayspring," appears in the Benedictus. This rising or dawning light promises to dispel completely the darkness and shadow of death hovering over the people. Both the image of the way as applied to John the Baptist and the image of Dayspring as applied to Jesus reflect the prophecy of Malachi. His message draws to a conclusion with the promise of a messenger to prepare the way before the Lord (Mal. 3:1). Then, to those who fear the name of the Lord, Malachi promises, "there will arise the sun of justice with its healing rays" (Mal. 3:20). This sunrise imagery along with the "horn of saving strength" (Lk. 1:69) were quite possibly symbols associated with the birth of the messiah. Ezechiel joined the two symbols when he prophesied that God would "cause to rise a horn for the house of Israel" (Ez. 29:21).[21] In working with the Malachi text, Luke associated peace with the rising sun rather than justice. Perhaps in the light of the strong justice themes of Mary's Magnificat, Luke deliberately identified the new way with peace, a peace which presupposes and depends on the "healing rays of justice." Justice, in turn, depends on peaceful conditions for the development of those relationships which satisfy human needs in both the personal and societal orders. In harmonizing the justice themes of Mary's song with the peace themes of both Zechariah's song and the angels', Lucan artistry is at work in echoing Psalm 85 once again, with its promise that "justice and peace shall kiss."

The fourth and final canticle in the Lucan infancy narrative is that of Simeon, that "just and pious" man who had long awaited "the consolation of Israel" (Lk. 2.25f). Attuned to the Holy Spirit, Simeon took Jesus in his arms and sang his small song of praise. Peace keynotes Simeon's canticle, the peace resulting from God's fulfillment of covenantal promises in sending the Messiah. How significant that Simeon described Jesus as the servant of Yahweh foretold by Isaiah as "a revealing light to the Gentiles, the glory of your people Israel" (Lk. 2:32; Is. 42:6; 49:6). Above all in this Canticle, Luke sounded the Isaian prophet servant motif which resounds through the third Gospel, from the baptism of Jesus (Lk. 3:22), to the Nazareth synagogue episode (Lk. 4:16f), to the transfiguration (Lk. 9:35), throughout the passion account, and finally culminates in the climactic question at Emmaus, "Did not the Messiah have to undergo all this so as to enter into his glory?" (Lk. 24:26). Simeon's heart-rending words to Mary accentuate the suffering servant theme and set the tone for Mary and for all faithful Christians to share the servant life of Jesus with all its peacemaking implications.

A Parallel Christology

The messianic Christology of Luke's infancy narrative with all its peacemaking overtones resonates with the incipient peacemaking Christology in the Epistle to the Ephesians. Both these sections of the New Testament are concerned with early Jewish-Christian relations. While questions of Ephesians' authorship remain unresolved, it is difficult to ascertain with certainty that the peacemaking Christological emphasis of Ephesians played a major role in the theological design of the Lucan infancy narrative. However, scholars seem to agree that the Epistle to the Ephesians is definitely Pauline in its theology, and was composed as a circular letter for several Churches. Quite possibly this letter was written during Paul's first Roman house arrest at a time when Luke may have been present.[22] In any event, both the Lucan infancy narrative and Ephesians are similar in their strong peacemaking emphasis.

Early on in its teachings, *The Challenge of Peace* refers to Ephesians three times. In the context of the "religious vision of peace among peoples and nations and the problems associated with realizing this vision . . . ," the Christological statement from Ephesians 2:14-16 is quoted in part. "Christ is our peace, for he has 'made us both one, and has broken down the dividing wall of hostility . . . that he might create in himself one new (person) in place of the two, so making peace, and might reconcile us both to God'" (#20). Then, in the New Testament section of this peace pastoral, we read, "Because the walls of hostility between God and humankind were broken down in the life and death of the true, perfect servant, union and well-being between God and the world were finally fully possible" (Eph. 2:13-22; Gal. 3:28) (#51). Another Ephesians reference pertains to the disciples of Jesus. "Discipleship reaches out to the ends of the earth and calls for reconciliation among all peoples so that God's purpose, 'a plan for the fullness of time, to unite all things in him' (Eph. 1:10) will be fulfilled" (#54).

It can hardly be overemphasized that *The Challenge of Peace* situates the Christological peacemaking theology of Ephesians in the context of today's warmaking world. Obviously, our present national "dividing walls of hostility" were not the original focus of the epistle. The immediate Pauline concern was the enmity between Jew and Gentile, and this enmity did have far-reaching repercussions in the political world of Paul's day. In Klassen's chapter on "Paul and the Good News of Peace," he stresses Paul's intent to consider peace and peacemaking in all human relations.[23] Referring directly to the Ephesians text (2:14-18), Klassen asserts, "No other statement so strongly affirms the central place which peace holds in Paul's thinking, and none is so clearly based in the nature, person, and work of Christ."[24] Furthermore this Ephesians text makes clear that the cross is the basis for Paul's teaching on peace.[25] ". . . You who once were far off have been brought near through the blood of Christ" (Eph. 2:13), who reconciled "both of us to God in one body through his cross . . . " (Eph. 2:16).

In this direct association of the suffering and death of Jesus with peacemaking, we are at the very heart of the Pauline peacemaking Christology. This theology teaches that Jesus, the anointed one, the Christ, entered into the existential situation of human hostility, enmity, divisiveness, and hatred and took it all unto himself, into his own body on the cross. In Jesus the Christ, God became immersed in the human condition in its state of alienation from all that makes for peace, for the wholeness and well-being of life in all its aspects — personal, societal and cosmic. Into this realm of darkness and death Jesus peacemaker brought the love of God with all its transforming power for a new humanity, for a new creation.[26] This transforming love of God in Christ Jesus is the new law, the new way. In his own person Jesus has destroyed the hostility of the former way (v. 15). "But now in Christ Jesus" (v. 13) reconciliation and peace are realized. His new creation is a new humanity empowered by his own Spirit to live in the way of God's own reconciling love. As Max Zerwick comments, "Here peace and love are anchored in such grounds of being as only God's wisdom could design, God's ominpotence create, Christ's love give effect to."[27]

Because God's love in Christ Jesus is able to transform all the enmity in the entire cosmos, the reconciling power of Jesus peacemaker is not limited to the enmity of Jew and Gentile in the early years of the church's life. The reconciling power of Jesus peacemaker can be operative in all situations of enmity, wherever and whenever the followers of Jesus freely enter into God's own way of transforming love.

One of the ways the Epistle to the Ephesians describes the transforming character of God's love is by describing a military armor in very different terms. As the letter comes to an end, Christians are exhorted to "draw your strength from the Lord and his mighty power" (Eph. 6:10). Then a series of transformed military imagery follows, not unlike the transformed sword and arrow of Isaiah's second servant song (Is. 49:2) already described in Chapter Three of this study. This new "armor of God" includes truth as a belt, justice as a breastplate, and the gospel of peace as footgear (Eph. 6:14,15). In referring to the significance of transformed military imagery, *The Challenge of Peace* quotes this Ephesians text in one of the peace pastoral's explanations concerned with undoing the image of a warrior God (#40, 41).

To appreciate the transformative character of Ephesians' military symbolism, one must compare it to the armor of God imagery in the Book of Wisdom wherein a vengeance theme predominates.[28] In sharp contrast, a spirit of vengeance is totally lacking in Ephesians, as it is in the Lucan Gospel.[29] Furthermore, Ephesians specifies the real enemy of peace in ways far more explicit than the Wisdom texts. "Our battle is not against human forces but against the principalities and powers, the rulers of this world of darkness, the evil spirits in regions above" (Eph. 6:12). Identifying this common enemy of all human life is a key factor in choosing the plan of action to be followed by all members of the one human family, now able to be fully reconciled and united in God's love through Christ Jesus.

For God's own transforming love to be truly operative in human life, a prayerful union with God is a necessity. Small wonder that the Epistle to the Ephesians begins and ends in prayer, in prayer for grace and peace, for love and faith (Eph. 1:2; 6:23). In fact, the entire first half of the letter (1:3-3:21) is made up of prayers.[30] As this first doctrinal section of the letter begins, the "God and Father of our Lord Jesus Christ" is praised for the wondrous blessings bestowed on the human family in Christ (1:3). Later, this first section comes to a conclusion in prayer that "the breadth and length and height and depth of Christ's love" be grasped fully (3:18). Then, the early church is given a glorious doxology, one emphasizing the universality of God's reconciling and transforming power. "To him whose power now at work in us can do immeasurably more than we ask or imagine — to him be glory in the church and in Christ Jesus through all generations, world without end. Amen"

This early peacemaking Christology of Ephesians has not been given much prominence thus far in the history of the church's theological development. A recent publication by Leopold Sabourin of basic Christological texts hardly mentions Ephesians at all. No explicit reference is made to the epistle's text naming Jesus our peace and our peacemaker through the shedding of his blood. In fact, Sabourin gives no attention whatsoever to the early Christological awareness of Jesus peacemaker.[31]

This apparent lack of development of Ephesians' basic Christological insight into Jesus peacemaker calls for some explanation. Early Trinitarian controversies focused attention on the philosophical ways of gaining some insight into Jesus, the Incarnate Word and Only-begotten Son of the Father. Also, as the Church moved more and more into the Greco-Roman world, justifications for warmaking soon replaced the peacemaking stance of the early Christian communities. A necessary peacemaking experiential base was lost for the kind of theologizing which could develop an authentic peacemaking Christology. Perhaps the new peacemaking efforts of so many

Christian communities today will enable a vital peacemaking Christology to develop, one which will explicate the profound cosmic vision of the Epistle to the Ephesians.

Early Sacramental Life

The prayerful emphasis of the Epistle to the Ephesians suggests that it was composed from a collection of prayers and homiletic instructions for early liturgies.[32] In tune with the liturgical catechesis of Ephesians, a brief consideration of early sacramental practice will be the final prelude of this study. Once again, the image of prelude can be helpful especially when the sacraments of baptism and eucharist are understood as sacraments of initiation, preluding a Christian way of life.

The peacemaking emphasis of the earliest centuries of Christian life suggests quite strongly that early sacramental instruction must have included the good news of peace and peacemaking as an integral part of this new way of life in Christ Jesus. Several texts from the first three centuries of the church's life indicate that Christians were seen as persons committed to peace, sometimes even to the witness of martyrdom. Often these early texts have direct allusions to baptism.

Perhaps the strongest testimony to the early Christian witness to peacemaking was in the practice of sacramental life. Tertullian claimed that the military oath (sacramentum) cannot be reconciled with the promise (sacramentum) made at baptism.[33] From a sacramental point of view, Tertullian's treatise, *On the Crown* (211 A.D.) raised pertinent questions with respect to a Christian in military service. Tertullian asked:

> Do we think that one can rightfully superimpose a
> human oath on one made to God? And that a man
> can answer to a second lord once he has acknow-
> ledged Christ? . . . Is it right to make a profession
> of the sword when the Lord has proclaimed that the

man who uses it will perish by it . . . a pretext like
this (military service) undercuts the whole meaning
of the baptismal oath.[34]

Tertullian's testimony on the incompatibility of military service and baptism is exemplified by the heroic witness of Maximilian, the first known conscientious objector. Near the end of
the third century this young man went to his death rather than
yield to the military demands of the proconsul Dion. Some of
the dialogue between Maximilian and Dion as recorded in the
Acts of the Christian Martyrs is pertinent. As Maximilian refused to be measured for a military uniform, he protested, "I
cannot serve in the army; I cannot engage in wrongdoing; I am
a Christian." When asked to accept the military seal, Maximilian responded, "I will not take it. I already have a seal, the
seal of Christ, my God . . . I am a Christian; I may not carry
a piece of lead around my neck now that I have accepted the
saving seal of my Lord Jesus Christ, son of the living God. You
know nothing about him, but he suffered for our salvation, and
he was delivered up by God for our sins. It is he whom all
Christians serve; it is he whom we follow as life's sovereign."[35]

Maximilian's convictions on the impossibility of reconciling
Christian life with military service correspond with the direc-
tives of some of the early Church Orders, those manuals of
discipline which could be considered forerunners of Canon Law.
Therein we find the directness of legal language in their pre-
scriptions forbidding baptized Christians to participate in army
life. The *Apostolic Tradition*, attributed to Hippolytus, attested
to early third century practice in Rome. Section XVI com-
manded, "A catechumen or a member of the faithful who wants
to join the army should be dismissed because he has shown
contempt for God."[36] Other documents developed during the
early Constantinian era in the outlying areas of the church.
The *Egyptian Church Order*, probably composed in the early
fourth century, gave this directive: "And a catechumen or believer, if they wish to be a soldier, shall be rejected, because it
is far from God."[37] *The Testament of Our Lord*, compiled in

Syria or in southeastern Asia Minor around the middle of the fourth century, stated emphatically, "Let a catechumen or a believer of the people, if he desire to be a soldier, either cease from his intention or if not let him be rejected."[38]

Not only was baptism considered incompatible with military service, but a eucharistic theology began to emerge which raised additional questions about the incongruity of Christians receiving the body and blood of Jesus and then proceeding to destroy the body and shed the blood of another person. One example of this emerging sacramental theology is found in the writings of St. Cyprian of Carthage. Cyprian in his treatise *On the Goodness of Patience* insisted that "after the reception of the eucharist the hand is not to be stained with the sword and bloodshed."[39]

These indications of a developing sacramental theology point indirectly to a developing Christology. Baptism was the beginning of a truly new life in Jesus. Participation in the sacred mysteries of the eucharist, the new covenant in Jesus' blood, made the violent shedding of blood in warfare absolutely unthinkable. If life in Jesus was such a new way, then an undaunted faith in the person of Jesus grounded that new way of seeing life.

Recalling Maximilian's testimony is helpful here. Refusing to join the Roman army, he professed Jesus Christ is "son of the living God . . . who suffered for our salvation, . . . whom we follow as life's sovereign and as the author of salvation."[40] Maximilian, hardly more than a teenager when he was martyred, is not considered one of the early church's theologians. But his profession of faith is true to the Gospel and also contains the substance of the later classic formulas of Nicea and Chalcedon which profess that Jesus is truly God and truly human. Furthermore, corresponding with much of our contemporary Christological emphases, Maximilian professed his faith in the salvific power of Jesus' real human sufferings.

To this day, Christians wrestle with the incompatibility of partaking in the eucharistic body and blood of Jesus and then proceeding to destroy the bodies and shed the blood of almost countless members of God's human family through modern warfare. Perhaps no contemporary writer has spoken more forcibly to this spirituality of outright contradiction than Daniel Berrigan in his commentary on the Lord's Prayer. His chapter entitled, "Give Us This Day Our Daily Bread" has manifold eucharistic implications and includes the following indictment.

> Most Americans would like to have the Pentagon and the welfare state, the bread basket and bomb turret both full, death and life feeding at the same table, wrestling it out on the same battlefield. We dream of some demonic marrriage between Christ and Baal. We love healthy bouncy children, we regretfully slaughter children. We want a stake in both sides of the Great Divide, the chasm set up between heaven and hell. Spiritually such an effort is absurd; the contradictions literally tear us apart; schizoid, a fair image of those who dwell not in both places, but simply in hell.[41]

One of the most crucial questions facing the church today is whether the prayer life of contemporary Christians is beginning to transform the consciences of those praying Christians with respect to warmaking and peacemaking. In her excellent commentary on *The Challenge of Peace*, Kathleen Hughes reminds us that the ancient church, especially in the East, saw the liturgy as its "first theology."[42] That is to say, the symbolic language of the liturgy gave the first expression to the community's self-understanding. Only then was a more speculative theology able to follow, a development also necessary to the faith life of the community.

Once more we can turn to the Epistle to the Ephesians and find a remarkable synthesis of the Church's understanding of the new peacemaking way of life in Christ Jesus. The Ephesians text on Jesus peacemaker not only relates its Christology to baptism, but clearly alludes to the eucharist with its reference to the blood of Jesus (Eph. 2:13). Such theological understanding depended on a vital liturgical life, one which celebrated sacraments in harmony with everyday Gospel living.

As we know from the early Church Orders, regulations for the liturgical life of the Church gave strong evidence of Christians seriously committed to Jesus' way of peace. If our "new moment" of human history is to recover Jesus' peacemaking way of life, then, like the early church, we must harmonize our peacemaking efforts with a prayer life really attuned to the Gospel. Scripture and sacrament remain our preludes to a peacemaking in union with Jesus peacemaker. Only as we enter more fully into this peacemaking way of life will we come to know Christ Jesus who "came and 'announced the good news of peace'" (Eph. 2:17).

Footnotes

[1] See Raymond Brown's helpful explanation in *The Birth of the Messiah* (Garden City, NY: Doubleday 1977) pp. 27-29 on "The Formation of the Gospels."

[2] Brown, *The Birth*, p. 242f.

[3] Brown, *The Birth*, p. 29f. Also consult Joseph A. Fitzmyer, *The Gospel According to Luke I-IX*, in *The Anchor Bible* (Garden City, NY: Doubleday 1981) p. 192f.

[4] Brown, *The Birth*, p. 253.

[5] Fitzmyer, *The Gospel*, pp. 309, 358. Brown, *The Birth* pp. 250-253.

[6] Fitzmyer, *The Gospel*, p. 358.

[7] Fitzmyer, *The Gospel*, p. 225. Also see William Klassen, *Love of Enemies* (Philadelphia: Fortress Press 1984) p. 80.

[8] Fitzmyer, *The Gospel*, p. 224. Klassen, *Love*, p. 82.

[9] Klassen, *Love*, p. 80.

[10] Arturo Paoli, *Meditations on St. Luke*, tr. Bernard F. McWilliams (Maryknoll: Orbis 1977) p. 185.

[11] Paoli, *Meditations*, p. 196.

[12] Philip and Sally Scharper, eds. *The Gospel in Art by the Peasants of Solentiname* (Maryknoll: Orbis 1984) p. 8.

[13] *Ibid*.

[14] Mary Donahey, "Mary, Mirror of Justice," in Carol Frances Jegen, ed., *Mary According to Women* (Kansas City: Sheed and Ward 1985) p. 76.

[15] Carol Frances Jegen, "Mary Immaculate, Woman of Freedom, Patroness of the United States," in Carol Frances Jegen, ed., *Mary*, p. 154.

[16] John R. Donahue, "Biblical Perspectives on Justice," in John C. Haughey, ed., *The Faith That Does Justice* (New York: Paulist Press 1977) p. 69.

[17] Cf. Joseph Jensen, *Isaiah 1-39* (Wilmington, DE: Michael Glazier, Inc. 1984) p. 110f.

[18] Fitzmyer, *The Gospel*, p. 379. Brown, *The Birth*, p. 379.

[19] Brown, *The Birth*, p. 390.

[20] Fitzmyer, *The Gospel*, p. 164f, and especially p. 169. For an interesting and timely discussion of some of the implications of Pauline "way theology" see Gustavo Gutierrez, *We Drink From Our Own Wells*, tr. Matthew J. O'Connell (Maryknoll: Orbis 1984) p. 80f.

[21] Brown, *The Birth*, p. 390f.

[22] Cf. Lionel Swain, *Ephesians* (Wilmington, DE: Michael Glazier, Inc. 1980) p. x. Maximilian Zerwick, *The Epistle to the Ephesians*, tr. Kevin Smyth (New York: Herder and Herder 1969) p. xii. Fitzmyer, *The Gospel*, pp. 37, 41.

[23] Klassen, *Love*, p. 124.

[24] Klassen, *Love*, p. 125.

[25] *Ibid.*

[26] Swain, *Ephesians*, p. 58.

[27] Zerwick, *The Epistle*, p. 66.

[28] Klassen, *Love*, p. 126f.

[29] Cf. Klassen, *Love*, p. 82f.

[30] Swain, *Ephesians*, p. x.

[31] Leopold Sabourin, *Christology: Basic Texts in Focus* (New York: Alba House 1984) p. 131f.

[32] Swain, *Ephesians*, pp. x, 4.

[33] Louis J. Swift, *The Early Fathers on War and Military Service* (Wilmington, DE: Michael Glazier, Inc. 1983) p. 42.

[34] Tertullian, *On the Crown*, as quoted in Swift, *The Early*, pp. 43-45.

[35] *Acts of Martyrs*, as quoted in Swift, *The Early*, p 72f.

[36] *Apostolic Tradition*, as quoted in Swift, *The Early*, p. 47.

[37] *Egyptian Church Order*, as quoted in C. John Cadoux, *The Early Christian Attitude to War* (London: Headly, 1919; rpt New York: Seabury 1982) pp. 122, 123. Also see Cadoux's remarks on p. 259.

[38] *Ibid.*

[39] Cyprian of Carthage, *Liber de Bono Patientiae*, as translated in Swift, *The Early*, p. 34. For a further analysis of this text along with a consideration of the impossibility of reconciling participation in the eucharist with participation in warfare, see my article, "The Eucharist and Peacemaking: Sign of Contradiction?" in *Worship* 59 (1985) pp. 202-210.

[40] Cf. note 35.

[41] Daniel Berrigan, *The Words Our Savior Gave Us* (Springfield: Templegate Publishers 1978) p. 88.

[42] Kathleen Hughes, "The Voice of the Church at Prayer: A Liturgical Appraissal," in John T. Pawlikowski and Donald Senior, eds.,*Biblical and Theological Reflections on The Challenge of Peace* (Wilmington, DE: Michael Glazier, Inc. 1984) p. 136. This article's juxtaposition of liturgical texts illustrating the Church's changing mentality toward war and peace provides extremely helpful examples of the possibilities inherent in liturgical prayer for conscience formation.